Anonymous

Phallism

A description of the worship of lingam-yoni in various parts of the world

Anonymous

Phallism
A description of the worship of lingam-yoni in various parts of the world

ISBN/EAN: 9783337282714

Printed in Europe, USA, Canada, Australia, Japan

Cover: Foto ©Andreas Hilbeck / pixelio.de

More available books at **www.hansebooks.com**

PHALLISM:

A DESCRIPTION OF THE WORSHIP

OF

LINGAM-YONI

IN VARIOUS PARTS OF THE WORLD, AND IN DIFFERENT
AGES, WITH AN ACCOUNT OF

ANCIENT & MODERN CROSSES

PARTICULARLY OF THE

CRUX ANSATA

(OR HANDLED CROSS)

AND OTHER SYMBOLS CONNECTED WITH THE MYSTERIES OF

SEX WORSHIP

London

PRIVATELY PRINTED

1889

PREFACE.

THE subject described and illustrated in the following pages, though springing from a common source, has naturally many branches, and assumes a number of somewhat complicated forms; in order, however, to keep the volume within its intended limits, care has been taken not to digress from the main topic, or stray in any way from the matter indicated by the title.

It may perhaps occur to a casual observer, that Phallism is a topic wanting in sufficient interest to make it worthy of any amount of consideration or study, it is hoped that the extraordinary facts here narrated, the extensive and tenacious hold this worship had and still has upon multitudes in various parts of the world, and the mysterious objects supposed to be connected with it, meeting us in all directions, will speedily dissipate such an idea. A subject which reaches from the earliest dawn of history through long and eventful ages, down to the most modern times, and touches almost every kingdom of the past and present, in the four quarters of the earth, and which is so closely interwoven with the moral, social, and religious life of the vast British dominions in the East, must have an interest peculiarly its own.

Still further, the discovery of the sites of ancient kingdoms, and the unearthing of long buried statues, monuments, and mystifying inscriptions, has suggested and provoked new lines of study amongst symbolical remains, and the key to so much that for long was unreadable, has been found in the singular revelations of this peculiar worship.

It is not pretended that such a treatise is of a nature which would render it suitable for the inspection of all ages and classes, there are numberless things constantly occurring about us which are wisely concealed from the young and inexperienced, but which it is necessary men of mature judgments should be acquainted with, but it will for the most part, be found after all, not so necessarily indelicate as some suppose, if properly viewed in connection with its own times and circumstances. That licentiousness and grossness have been intimately associated with it at certain times and in certain places, is undeniable, but there are facts in history which the faithful chronicler is bound to exhibit and narrate as far as possible in a manner consistent with the more refined and polished manners of the age. In such style we have endeavoured to tell our story and in commending its strange revelations to our readers, we can only remind them of the old and familiar motto, "Evil be to him that evil thinks."

CONTENTS.

Horace's Satire on Priapus.
Belphegor.
Excesses during the Worship of Priapus.
Roman Priapus derived from the Egyptians.
Catullus on the Worship of Priapus.
Various Priapian Forms.
Phallism in Various Countries.
St. Augustine.
St. Foutin and Priapus.
French Phallism.
Neapolitan Festivals.
Maypoles in India and England.

Phallic Worshippers of the East.
Linga Described.
Caves of Elephanta.
Lucian and the Temple at Hierapolis.
Small Linga.
Ceremony of Linga-puja.
Woman at Worship described.
Hindu Desire for Children.
The Temple of Nuptials.
Reproach attached to Barren Women.
Story of Shravana and Dasaratha.
The Twelve Lingas.
Distinction between Linga and Yoni.
Argha.
Veneration for Stones.
Story of Polluted Brahmans.
Brahmans and Fire Production.
Feuds between the Linga and Yoni Worshippers.
Legend of Sarti and Parvati.

Legend concerning Mahadeva.
Diodorus Siculus on Osiris.
Ptolemy Philadelphus.
The Vaishnavas.
Hindu Sects.
Worship of Female Generative Principle.

PHALLISM.

CHAPTER I.

*Nature and origin of the subject—Peculiarity of the subject—
Definition of Phallic Worship—Phallaphoroi—Antiquity of
Phallic Worship — The Primitive Oath — Pegasus and the
Statues of Bacchus—Sheevah and Prakreety, a Legend—Feast
of the Funeral Pile — Lucian and the Syrian Goddess —
Common Origin of Pagan beliefs — Pagan Rites involved in
obscurity — Phallic Objects in Dahome — Development of
Phallism—Innocent Origins—Extravagances connected with
Phallism—Superstitious usages in England—Cleft Trees and
Physical Infirmities.*

THE subject before us is of so remarkable a character, and so
surrounded with the mystical and the unlikely, that, but
for an abundance of incontrovertible facts supported by the
investigations of accurate observers, and an almost unlimited
number of ancient monuments and emblems, we should be disposed to put it aside as too mythical and uncertain to be worth
our serious attention. Whatever we may think of it, however,
whatever may be the mystery surrounding its origin, and whatever the extravagances of the views of development theorists,
who have professed to discern in it the germs of even the highest
forms of modern worship, it is a fact beyond contradiction that
it has prevailed and still prevails to a very large extent in certain
parts of the world, and must be regarded as the most ancient
form of natural religion known.

By phallic worship we mean the adoration of the generative
organs as symbols of the creative powers of nature. The word
is a Greek one (*Phallos*), and is interpreted as representing the

B

membrum virile, especially a figure thereof which was carried in
procession in the Bacchic orgies, as an emblem of the generative
power in nature.   Other and kindred words found in the same
language refer variously to a similar thing, thus :—*Phallephoria*,
a festival of Bacchus in which a phallus was carried in procession ; *Phallikos*, belonging to the phallic festivals ; *Phallobates*,
a phallic priest ; and *Ithyphalloi*, men disguised as women, who
followed immediately behind the phallus in the Greek processions
of the Dionysia.   Then we get *Phallaphoroi*, a name given at
Sicyon to certain mimes who ran about the streets smutted with
black and clothed in sheepskins, bearing baskets full of various
herbs—as violet, ivy, &c.—and bearing the phallus made of red
leather.   The word is from *Phallos*, a pole at the end of which
was fastened the figure of a human penis, and *Phero*, I bear.

Two things chiefly impress themselves upon our attention in
this study : the great antiquity of phallic worship, and the
extensive degree in which it has for ages prevailed in certain
parts of the world, especially in India.

With regard to its antiquity, it is impossible to assign any date
with certainty respecting its origin and rise.   Some do not
hesitate to describe it as the most ancient form of faith that we
know of ; and as a system of natural religion, probably, as we
have already said, that is true.   Richard Gough, in his *Comparative View of the Ancient Monuments of India* (London,
1785), said :—" Those who have penetrated into the abstruseness
of Indian Mythology find that in these temples was practised a
worship similar to that practised by all the several nations of the
world, in their earliest as well as their most enlightened periods.
It was paid to the phallus by the Asiatics ; to Priapus by the
Egyptians, Greeks, and Romans ; to Baal-Peor by the Canaanites
and idolatrous Jews.   The figure is seen on the fascia which
runs round the circus of Nismes, and over the portal of the

cathedral of Toulouse and several churches of Bordeaux. M. d'Ancarville has written two large quarto volumes to prove phallic worship to be the most ancient idea of the deity. This latter writer, indeed, along with others who have dealt with the subject, affirmed that the death and deification of Brama, called the " Gracious One," or " Prince of Peace," " Siva," or " Maha- deva," took place 3553 B.C. Forlong, in his *Rivers of Life*, endeavours again and again to show that phallic worship is far more ancient than any other religion known ; and he says in one place (Vol. 2, page 38) :— " The earliest instance I know of phallic worship or reverence, or at all events of phallic drawings, is that mentioned in the *Moniteur* of January, 1865. There it is related that in the province of Venetia, Italy, in a bone cave beneath ten feet of stalagmite, and amidst post-tertiary remains, beside a bone needle, was found a rude drawing of a phallus, scratched on a plate of an argillaceous compound, surely a very primeval idea of the Linga-in-Argha."

In harmony with the difficulty of fixing upon dates is the further difficulty of tracing the origin of this kind of worship. Dr. Ginsburg, in the article " Oath " in Kitto's Cyclopedia, finds reverence for the phallus, if not worship, in primitive customs as old as the time of Abraham. He says :—" Another primitive custom which obtained in the patriarchal age was that the one who took the oath ' put his hand under the thigh ' of the adjurer (Gen. 24, 2, 47, 29). This practice evidently arose from the fact that the genital member, which is meant by the euphemic expres- sion, ' thigh,' was regarded as the most sacred part of the body, being the symbol of union in the tenderest relation of matri- monial life, and the seat whence all issue proceeds, and the perpetuity so much coveted by the ancients (comp. Gen. 46, 26 ; Exod. 1, 5 ; Judges, 8, 30). Hence this creative organ became the symbol of the Creator, and the object of worship among all nations of antiquity; and it is for this reason that God claimed it as the sign of the covenant between Himself and His chosen people in the rite of circumcision. Nothing, therefore, could render the oath more solemn in those days than touching the symbol of creation, the sign of the covenant, and the source of that issue who may, at any future period, avenge the breaking of a compact made with their progenitor."

One account of the origin of the phallica, or feasts and sacrifices celebrated at Athens in honour of Bacchus (gathered chiefly from Aristophanes) is to the effect that one Pegasus, a native of Cleutheris, in Bœotia, having brought to Athens some statues of Bacchus, was treated by the Athenians with the utmost contempt and ridicule. The deity, indignant at the insult, in revenge sent among them an epidemic disease, which attacked them in their private organs. On consulting the oracle upon the best method of preventing the further extension of so grievous a malady, they were recommended publicly to receive Bacchus into their city in all the pomp of his worship. The oracle was obeyed, and amidst other splendid trophies, to appease the incensed divinity, were displayed thyrsi, with the figures of the parts affected bound to the end of them. M. Bochart, and Bishop Patrick in his commentary on I. Samuel, 5 and 6, curtly pronounce this story to be a forgery from a passage in the latter book, where the Philistines, having taken and violated the Ark of the God of Israel, are smitten with emerods, a distemper concerning the exact nature of which the commentators are not fully agreed, but which has been supposed to be of the same nature with that before mentioned. On inquiry of the priests with what trespass-offering the God of Israel might be appeased, they were directed, among other things, to prepare five golden emerods, according to the number of the principal cities of Philistia, and dedicate them to the God of Israel; which mandate when they had obeyed, the distemper ceased to make further ravages among them. There is great similarity in these two accounts, it is true, but that by no means implies that there has been a forgery, as it is well known that the ancient heathen consecrated to their gods such memorials of their deliverance as best represented the evils from which they were liberated, and it is a custom to this day for the pilgrim, when he goes to a pagoda for the cure of any disease, to bring the figure of the member affected, made either of gold, silver, or copper, according to his rank and ability, as an offering to the god.*

There is a Hindoo legend which explains the matter as follows, and which some regard as similar to the above :—Certain devotees in a remote time had acquired great renown and respect, but the purity of the heart was wanting ; nor did their motives and secret thoughts correspond with their professions and exterior conduct. They affected poverty, but were attached to the things of this world; and the princes and nobles were constantly sending them offerings. They seemed to sequester themselves from the world, they lived retired from the towns, but their dwellings were commodious and their women numerous and handsome. But nothing can be hid from the gods, and Sheevah resolved to expose them to shame. He desired Prakreety (Nature) to accompany him, and assumed the appearance of a Pandaram of a graceful form. Prakreety appeared as a damsel of matchless beauty. She went where the devotees were assembled with their disciples, waiting the rising sun to perform their ablutions and religious ceremonies. As she advanced, the refreshing breeze, moving her flowing robe, showed the exquisite shape which it seemed intended to conceal. With eyes cast down, though sometimes opening with a timid but a tender look, she approached them, and with a low enchanting voice desired to

* Tavernier.—*Voyage aux Indes.*

be admitted to the sacrifice. The devotees gazed on her with astonishment. The sun appeared, but the purifications were forgotten; the things for the Pooja lay neglected; nor was any worship thought of but that to her. Quitting the gravity of their manners, they gathered round her as the flies round the lamp at night, attracted by its splendour but consumed by its flame. They asked from whence she came, whither she was going. " Be not offended with us for approaching thee, forgive us for our importunities. But thou art incapable of anger, thou who art made to convey bliss; to thee, who mayest kill by indifference, indignation and resentment are unknown. But whoever thou mayest be, whatever motive or accident may have brought thee amongst us, admit us into the number of thy slaves, let us at least have the comfort to behold thee."

Here the words faltered on the lip, the soul seemed ready to take its flight; the vow was forgotten, and the policy of years was destroyed.

Whilst the devotees were lost in their passions and absent from their homes, Sheevah entered their village with a musical instrument in his hand, playing and singing like some of those who solicit charity. At the sound of his voice the women immediately quitted their occupations, they ran to see from whence it came. He was beautiful as Krishen (the Apollo of the Hindoos) on the plains of Matra. Some dropped their jewels without turning to look for them; others let fall their garments, without perceiving that they discovered those abodes of pleasure which jealousy, as well as decency, has ordered to be concealed. All pressed forward with their offerings, all wished to speak, all wished to be taken notice of, and bringing flowers and scattering them before him, said :—" Askest thou alms, thou who art made to govern hearts? Thou whose countenance is fresh as the morning, whose voice is the voice of pleasure, and thy breath like that of Vassant (Spring) in the opening rose! Stay with us and we will serve thee, nor will we trouble thy repose, but only be jealous how to please thee!"

The Pandaram continued to play, and sung the loves of Kama, of Krishen, and the Gopia; and smiling the gentle smiles of fond desire he led them to a neighbouring grove that was consecrated to pleasure and retirement. *Soav* (the sun) began to gild the western mountains, nor were they offended at the retiring day.

But the desire of repose succeeds the waste of pleasure. Sleep closed the eyes, and lulled the senses. In the morning the Pandaram was gone. When they awoke they looked round with astonishment, and again cast their eyes upon the ground. Some directed their looks to those who had been formerly remarked for their scrupulous manners, but their faces were covered with their veils. After sitting awhile in silence they arose, and went back to their houses with slow and troubled steps. The devotees returned about the same time from their wanderings after Prakreety. The days that followed were days of embarrassment and shame. If the women had failed in their modesty the devotees had broken their vows. They were vexed at their weakness, they were sorry for what they had done; yet the tender sigh sometimes broke forth, and the eye often turned to where the men first saw the maid, the women the Pandaram.

But the people began to perceive that what the devotees foretold came not to pass. Their disciples, in consequence, neglected to attend them, and the offerings from the princes and the nobles became less frequent than before. They then performed various penances; they sought for secret places among the woods, unfrequented by man; and having at last shut their eyes from the things of this world, and retired within themselves in deep meditation, they discovered that Sheevah was the author of their misfortunes. Their understanding being imperfect, instead of bowing the head with humility they were inflamed with anger; instead of contrition for their hypocrisy they sought for vengeance. They performed new sacrifices and incantations, which were only allowed to have effect in the end to show the extreme folly of man in not submitting to the will of heaven. Their incantations produced a tiger, whose mouth was like a cavern, and his voice like thunder among the mountains. They sent him against Sheevah, who, with Prakreety, was amusing himself in the vale. He smiled at their weakness, and killing the tiger at one blow with his club, he covered himself with his skin. Seeing themselves frustrated in this attempt the devotees had recourse to another, and sent serpents against them of the most deadly kind. But on approaching him they became harmless, and he twisted them round his neck. They then sent their curses and imprecations against him, but they all recoiled upon themselves. Not yet disheartened by all these disappointments, they collected all their prayers, their penances, their charities, and other good works, the most acceptable of all sacrifices, and demanding in return only vengeance against Sheevah, they sent a consuming fire to destroy his genital parts. Sheevah, incensed at this attempt, turned the fire with indignation against the human race, and mankind would soon have been destroyed, had not Vishnu, alarmed at the danger, implored him to suspend his wrath. At his entreaties Sheevah relented. But it was ordained that in his temples those parts should be worshipped which the false devotees had impiously attempted to destroy.

The author of *Indian Antiquities* observes:—"Possibly in Syria is to be found the genuine origin both of the Indian and Egyptian phallic worship."

Lucian's tract on the Syrian Goddess is regarded by scholars as of particular value in matters belonging to the religions of the ancients, as it contains an accurate detail of the superstitious rites celebrated in the most remote periods and in the most renowned pagan temples in the world. In the course of it he informs us that the grandest and most solemn feast observed by the ancient Syrians was known as " The Funeral Pile," or " The Torch " (some translate it " The Feast of Fire.") It was celebrated at Hierapolis at the commencement of the vernal season, and the sacrifices were of the most extravagant description. Everything was on a scale of the greatest magnitude and splendour, multitudes flocking from all parts of the adjacent countries, bringing their gods with them, to heighten the grandeur of the festival. The most remarkable feature of the proceedings, however, was that after the priests had been flogging and slashing each other with knives, some of them sacrificed to their protectress not the symbolical but the real phallus. A young man would be seized with a sudden fury, would tear the clothes from his back, leap amongst the assembled Galli, snatch up a short sword that had probably been long kept there for the purpose, castrate himself, run with what he had cut off round the city, go into whatever house the fancy took him to throw it, from which house he was provided with a complete suit of woman's apparel, and all the ornaments becoming a lady.

This practice can only be accounted for either by that ancient maxim of superstition that whatsoever is most sacredly precious to mankind should be consecrated to the gods, and that we please them best when we make the most costly sacrifice ; by supposing that, in the perpetration of an act so abhorrent to nature, they intended to give public proof of a vow of perpetual virginity, or on account of a particular mythological reason.

Those mythologists who consider the Syrian goddess to be a personification of the earth, as Cybele in Greece doubtless was, rather than of nature, insist that eunuch-priests allude to the barren state of that earth wtihout cultivation. When considered in this point of view, they represent the noise of her beaten cymbals, which denote the globe, as allusive to the uproar which

the warring winds, waters, and subterraneous fires confined in its
cavities, occasion, and which, convulsing its internal regions,
produce earthquakes and volcanic eruptions; and the rattling of
her brazen sistra they understand as figurative of the clashing of
the various instruments used in husbandry, which were in the
first instance composed of brass.   It is indeed a principal object
with Lucian in his treatise to demonstrate that Rhea of Greece
was the Dea Syria of the Babylonians; in this he may be right,
since the very same species of worship, and the use of the very
same instruments have immemorially prevailed in India.   His
hypothesis, if admitted, only exhibits still more glaring proof
how universally throughout the pagan world a system of gross
physics prevailed, and the earth was adored instead of its Creator.

Many, however, are inclined to the opinion of other mythologists, who consider this celebrated deity, in the most extensive
view of her character, as *universal nature* herself, which includes
not only the earth but the whole circle of being; and though,
when understood in this point of view, the mutilation of her
priests may appear somewhat singular, there was another custom
practised in her temple very consonant to this character, the
consideration of which brings us back to the dancing girls of
India, who were public prostitutes, and were denominated women
of the idol.   This custom, recorded with expressions of indignation by Herodotus, was that all female votaries of this deity,
once at least in their lives, should prostitute themselves to some
stranger in the polluted porches of this temple.   It had, says
that historian, for this infamous purpose, a long range of galleries
open on every side, that the passing stranger might more freely
view the assembled fair, thus devoutly frail, and make his choice
with unrestrained freedom.   For the object of his choice he did
not, like the proud sultan, throw the handkerchief of love, but a
piece of silver coin, into her lap, which the severe laws of the

country forbade her to refuse, as well as his embrace, however disgusting might be her lover. The wages of iniquity, thus menially obtained, were accounted holy, and were devoted to increase the treasures of the temple. Every female in that district, without exception, the noble as well as ignoble, the princess and the peasant's wife, were alike obliged to go through this indispensable ceremony of initiation into the mysteries of Mylitta; with this difference only, that women of distinguished rank, with a numerous train of servants attending at some little distance, no doubt with the politic intention to overawe any intruder of mean parentage from approaching the shrine of princely beauty, took their station in covered chariots at the gate. Such were the rites of the Syrian goddess, and the reader, by comparing the account with those of the Bayaderes, will find that the devotees of India were by no means behind those of Syria in the duty of sacrificing at the shrine of nature, either at the vernal or autumnal equinox.*

Faber, in his *Origin of Pagan Idolatry*, says (1 p. 58, &c.):—
" All the various modifications of paganism in every quarter of the globe originated from a common source, not from independent sources. . . . Each nation was thought to have its own ritual and its own set of deities, framed independently of every other nation, and if any coincidence were accidentally observed, it was deemed the effect of pure accident, not of design. In short, paganism was supposed to have as many different origins as there were nations which had apostatised from the truth." Further, he says:—" I will readily allow that if the premises were well founded the conclusion would be inevitable; that is to say, if the theological systems of the various pagan nations resembled each other only in what was *arbitrary*, and *circumstantial*, and *artificial*, we might be perfectly sure that they did not originate

* Maurice.—*Ind. Antiq.*

from any common source, but on the contrary that they were invented severally by each people after their settlement in their own particular country. The very reverse, however, of this will be found to be the case. The fact is that the various theological systems of the Gentiles agree not only in what is *obvious* and *natural*, but in what is *arbitrary* and *circumstantial*. There is such a singular, and minute, and regular accordance between them, both in *fanciful speculation* and in artificial observances, that no person who takes the pains of thoroughly investigating the subject, can avoid being fully persuaded that they must all have sprung from some common origin." The conclusion he comes to is that " all nations were once assembled together in a single place and in a single community, whence they adopted a corrupt form of religion, which they afterwards respectively carried with them into the lands that they colonised."

Despite all the speculation which has been indulged in respecting the origin of phallic worship, we are painfully conscious that no certain conclusion has yet been arrived at. Speaking generally, we can of course discern the leading idea involved in it—the intense desire of the Eastern to raise up a family, and his consequent veneration of those organs by whose powers alone his wishes could be fulfilled. For want of better knowledge his worship was natural and reasonable, and no doubt was perfectly free from everything that was immoral and licentious. Observing the creative power of the generative organs, seeing there the means of bringing forth beings like himself, with faculties of reasoning and thought, and religious conception, what wonder that he should render to them direct adoration, or should regard them as the types of the unknown and omnipotent Author of all things, his own and the world's Creator.

Mr. R. F. Burton, in his paper read before the Anthropological Society (Vol. 1, No. 10), on *Certain Matters connected with the Dahoman*, says :—" Amongst all barbarians, whose primal want is progeny, we observe a greater or a less development of the phallic worship. In Dahome it is uncomfortably prominent; every street from Whydah to the capital is adorned with the symbol, and the old ones are not removed. The Dahoman Priapus is a clay figure of any size between a giant and the pigmy, crouched upon the ground as if contemplating its own attributes. The head is sometimes a wooden block, rudely carved, more often dried mud, and the eyes and teeth are supplied by cowries. A huge penis, like the section of a broomstick, rudely carved, projects horizontally from the middle. I could have carried off a donkey's load had I been aware of the rapidly rising value of phallic specimens amongst the collectors of Europe. The Tree of Life is anointed with palm oil, which drips into a pot or a shard placed below it, and the would-be mother of children prays that the great god Legba will make her fertile. Female Legbas are rare, about one to a dozen males. They are if possible more hideous and gorilla-like than those of the other sex; their breasts resemble the halves of German sausages, and the external labia, which are adored by being anointed with oil, are painfully developed. There is another phallic god, named ' Bo,' the guardian of warriors and the protector of markets."

Originally, phallic worship had no other meaning than the allegorical one of that mysterious union between the male and the female which throughout nature seems to be the sole condition of the continuation of the existence of animated beings.* There is no reason whatever for supposing that licentiousness invented the rites incidental to the worship of Pan, Priapus, Bacchus, and Venus, whatever use may have been made of them afterwards. "It is impossible to believe," said Voltaire, "that depravity of manners would ever have led among any people to the establishment of religious ceremonies, though our ideas of

* Chambers.

propriety may lead us to suppose that ceremonies which appear to us so infamous could only be invented by licentiousness. It is probable that the first thought was to honour the deity in the symbol of life, and that the custom was introduced in times of simplicity." This is just how the matter strikes a thoughtful mind—that veneration and gratitude for the bounties of nature were thus expressed in ascriptions of praise, and humble dependence upon the deity for all good things in actions of sacrifice and supplication; in the course of time, however, the dangers attendant upon such a system developed themselves first into a wild enthusiasm, then into an extravagant mysticism, and finally into the practice of the most flagrant excesses, excesses so immoral and so opposed to the safety and well-being of society, that even in Rome, when it was the hot-bed of all sorts of unnatural vices, the senate had to interfere and put a check upon them. The Bacchic phrenzies were accordingly suppressed or mitigated as to their ostensible usages and tangible abominations. Nature, in the phraseology of certain sects, was no longer propitiated through the indulgence of feelings of her own prompting, excited further by the presence of unequivocal exhibitions. She, still personified, was more decently represented by certain symbols substituted for the earlier types; the cunning priests, no longer daring to exhibit their obscenities in shameless nudity, permitted only a portion of indecency to remain in the hands and eyes of their deluded votaries, and concealed their origin and meaning in the various mysteries and hieroglyphics denominated Bacchic, Eleusinian, Phallus, Linga, Yoni, &c.

By such people Nature was contemplated chiefly under her attribute or property of fecundity, and symbols of generative allusion were those under which her prolific potencies were exhibited. Those prone, like the Hindoos, to resolve almost everything into sexual allegory, of course fancied the male and female pudenda omni-archetypal. These, in the early days of such devotion, were probably pourtrayed in India, as elsewhere, without reserve; but were in most cases soon corrected into the comparative decency of the hieroglyphics; and the deluded people were cajoled by mummery and mystery that became less and less understood, and therefore, perhaps, the more reverenced. We have said in most cases, for in Egypt and Greece the grossness of phallism is known only in the remains of antiquity; in India it doubtless exists, but divested of obtrusive or conspicuous indelicacy; and too true it is that among Christians was the primeval infamy of the symbol and usage most tenaciously retained.*

According to M. Sonnerat, the professors of this worship were of the purest principles and the most unblemished conduct; and however offensive the idea may have proved to Europeans, it seems never to have entered into the heads of the Indian people that anything natural could be grossly obscene, "a singularity," observes Sir W. Jones, "which pervades all their writings and conversation, but which is no proof of depravity in their morals."

The student of this subject, whatever he may think of the apparently ridiculous and indecent ceremonies connected with it, will be forcibly struck with its almost universal presence in bygone ages, phallic monuments and emblems literally abounding in countries where anything religious has ever been professed. No doubt extravagances have been committed by many who have written upon the matter, resulting in the pretended discovery of images of the phallus in the most unlikely ornaments and parts of buildings erected for far different purposes, but the fact remains that such objects, of every conceivable size, have been met with by thousands in places where sex-worship was

* Rees.

practised, and apparently entering into the composition of ecclesiastical furniture and symbols used in the rites of religion of a more intellectual character. Leaving out of the case altogether such things as could only by the widest stretch of the imagination on the part of people anxious to sustain a theory be set up as phallic, we shall find especially, though not exclusively, in eastern nations full evidence of the vast extent to which the worship in question prevailed. In the course of this treatise we shall have occasion to call attention to some of the objects whose reputedly phallic character seems to us very far-fetched, if not altogether absurd, but we have no doubt whatever that the early religions of Egypt, India, Assyria, Greece, Spain, the Teutonic, Scandinavian, and other nations, most decidedly embodied as essential features, the worship of the sexual organs, the emblems of which are found by thousands. What, however, shall we say of the imagination which so runs to riot in seeking the typical and emblematic that the mouth of a cave, a fissure in the rocks, a perforation worn by the action of the waves, a promontory of land projecting from a continent, and even the human tongue protruded from the mouth, are regarded as figures either of the male or female organs, or of both in union! Yet so it is, and a cleft in the rock at the extremity of a bold headland in Barbary, called Malabar Point, is a celebrated Ioni, and passing through it is, and has been immemorially, a regenerating process.

Even England is not free from this superstition, and cases in both ancient and modern times are on record in which children have been passed through clefts in trees in order to cure them of their physical disorders; and it is a fact borne witness to by Dr. Borlase the author of the *History of Cornwall*, that there is a stone in the parish of Mardon, with a hole in it fourteen inches in diameter, through which many persons had crept for the relief of pains in the back and limbs, and through which also children had been drawn to cure them of the rickets.

By a singular coincidence, while the above was penning in reference to passing children through clefts in trees as a curative process for physical ailments, a report of such a case was actually printing in the *London Standard* newspaper, so that here in England, in the month of September 1888, the strange practice still survives. A correspondent of the above paper writes on the 27th of the month that such a case had come under his notice more than thirty years ago, while resident in Rio Janeiro, and that it was the only one he had heard of till the present one. Now some years back the practice was by no means uncommon in some parts of England, particularly in Suffolk; but, as Moor remarks in his *Oriental Fragments*, in comparison with India there was a considerable difference, in the latter country the process being regarded as spiritual, while in England, in 1834, it had become exclusively corporeal. More than a hundred years ago we find Cullum, in his *Antiquities of Hawstead*, writing:— "There is no place properer than this where I may mention a custom which I have twice seen practised within a few years, namely, that of drawing a child through a cleft tree. For this purpose a young ash tree was each time selected, and split longitudinally about five feet. The fissure was kept wide open by my gardener, while the friend of the child, having first stripped him, passed him thrice through it, always head foremost. As soon as the operation was performed the wounded tree was bound up with packthread, and as the bark healed the child was to recover. The first of these young patients was to be cured of the rickets, the second of a rupture," similar to the case reported in the *Standard*. "About the former," continues Cullum, "I had no opportunity of making any enquiry, but I frequently saw the father of the latter, who assured me that his child, without any other assistance, gradually mended, and at last grew perfectly well."

The author of the *Hindoo Fragments*, further says:—" The subject was recalled to my recollection by my bailiff when walking through a plantation in Woodbridge. I observed him rather minutely inspecting a young ash tree; and also looking, I saw it had a straight seam or scar, three feet or more in length. On my endeavouring to trace the cause, he told me that a child had been passed through the tree, split and opened for the purpose, to cure its rupture. The tree is not now so thick as one's wrist, and was not, when the ceremony was performed, above an inch in diameter. The impression is that as the tree heals of its wound, so will the child's ailment be removed. Great confidence seems to be placed in the mysterious efficacy of the process."

CHAPTER II.

Variations of Detail—The Egyptian Khem—Growing Coarseness of the Egyptian Idea—Swearing by the Phallus—Welsh Customs—The Hermaphroditic Element—Expressive Character of the Phallus—Phallic Emblems in Modern Times—Herodotus and the Bacchic Orgies—Priapus in Rome and Greece— Maachah a Worshipper of Priapus—Horace's Satire on Priapus—Belphegor—Excesses during the worship of Priapus —Roman Priapus derived from the Egyptians—Catullus on the worship of Priapus—Various Priapian Forms—Phallism in various Countries—St. Augustine—St. Foutin and Priapus —French Phallism—Neapolitan Festivals—Maypoles in India and England.

ALTHOUGH we shall have no difficulty in showing the similarity of pagan systems in all parts of the world, indicating to a very great extent a common origin, we are quite aware that in matters of detail considerable variations have ensued. The act or principle of which the phallus was the type was represented by a deity to whom it was consecrated, and in different nations this deity was known by various names. Thus, in Egypt we find Khem, the generative principle, supposed to be, indeed generally regarded as, the same as the Grecian Pan. "Khem," says Wilkinson, "from his character as a god of generation, was naturally looked upon as the deity to whose influence everything was indebted for its procreation, and for the continuation of its species; and we therefore frequently find in the sacred sculptures of Egyptian temples, the emblematic representation of a king breaking up the soil with a hoe, in the presence of this god, as if to prepare it for his beneficent influence. And this allegorical mode of worship was offered him, as well in

his character of Khem as when under the name of Amunra
Generator, which was one of the forms of the Theban Jupiter.
In the form of the god of generation originated, no doubt, the
Greek and Roman custom of placing their gardens under the
protection of Priapus, though instead of an abstract notion of the
generative influence, they, as in many other instances, merely
attached to it an idea according with the grossness of their
imagination."

Diodorous says that this god was held in great veneration by
the Egyptians, who not only set up images and statues in every
temple, but built a city in Thebides after his name, called by the
inhabitants Chemmin, or Cham, which is by interpretation Pan's
city.

The phallic worship of ancient Egypt appears to have been
characterised by certain notions of propriety which, in after years
and in other countries, were altogether regarded as superfluous.
Thus it was, in Egypt, the masculine members only which they
attempted to depict, and which formed such conspicuous features
in their statues and temples. "Their phallic exhibition," says
Bonwick, "was coarse, however, but forcible, and they, the
Egyptians, were the most natural in their portrayal. Nothing
could be plainer than the Ammon Generator, Ptah embryonic,
and ithyphallic Osiris. The generative force and activity of
deity could have no more striking a symbol."

An allusion was made in an early page to the subject of
eastern oaths, and it was pointed out that the putting the hand
upon the thigh was really putting it upon the private member,
and was the most solemn form of oath it was possible to take.
Nor has that custom yet died out in Egypt, for we are assured
by modern travellers that the Arabs, when desirous of forcibly
emphasising their words, or of giving unusual solemnity to them,
frequently so place their hands. A case in point has been quoted
occasionally by various writers from a letter of the Adjutant-

General Julian to a member of the Institute of Egypt (from the *Memoires sur l'Egypte, publiés pendant les Campagne de Bonaparte*), in which an Egyptian, who had been arrested as a spy and brought before the General, finding that all his protestations of innocence were not understood, uncovered himself and seized his private organ in his hand, again in a dramatic fashion affirming on oath that he was not what they took him to be.

Antiquarians say that some similar custom once prevailed in the northern parts of Europe, and that an ancient Welsh law, still extant, proves such to have been the case. This decree, from the laws of Hoel the Good, enacted that in a case of the forcible carnal knowledge of a woman, if the injured party desired justice on the offender, she must, when swearing to his identity, lay her right hand upon the relics of the saints, and with her left one grasp the member of the accused. As showing the antiquity of this practice amongst the Egyptians, Caylus gives in his Vol. 6 a plate representing Osiris grasping his phallus while taking an oath.

The more carefully ancient pagan systems of religion are regarded, the more evident will it become that sex-worship lay at the basis of all. " The hermaphroditic element of religion is sex-worship. Gods are styled ' he-she.' Synesius gives an inscription on an Egyptian deity :—' Thou art the father and thou art the mother—Thou art the male and thou art the female.' It was a son of Mercury and Venus that loved the nymph Salmacis, who, embracing him, begged the gods to make them one, and so a being hermaphroditic was formed."*

We get, it must be observed, in this phallus of Egyptian theology, two ideas practically, though they are nominally one. It exhibited the creative or regenerative power of deity, and the production of life from death, the renewal of being in other forms—in fact, resurrection. So it was painted on the ancient

* Bonwick.

coffin, and cut upon the tomb.   It was intended to convey to the
onlooker the idea of immortality; to remind him that though
the body was inanimate and dead, the spirit still survived.   As
Mariette Bey said, " These images only symbolised in a very
expressive manner the creative force of nature, without obscene
intention.   It was another way to express Celestial Generation,
which should cause the deceased to enter into a new life !

" The existence of a Creator could be illustrated by a potter at
the wheel.   But there was a much more expressive form familiar
to them, indicative of cause and effect in the production of births
in the tribe, or in nature around.   In this way the phallus
became the exponent of creative power, and, though to our eyes
vulgar and indecent, bore no improper meaning to the simple
ancient worshipper."*

Say what we will, think what we may of sex-worship, however
repulsive to our modern refined and cultivated tastes it may
appear, it was not only one of the most ancient forms of worship
but was the most natural way of expressing the idea of creation
and human dependence upon Providence, of the principle of
renewal and reproduction.   And it is not by our modern
standards its decency or indecency is to be judged ; the people
and their times must be taken into due and reasonable consideration, as we should do in endeavouring to form a just estimate of
customs and language once common in our own land.   Strangely
enough, many of the ancient symbols belonging to this worship
have been retained by ourselves to this very day, and are to be
found adorning some of the noblest churches of our land.   The
pinnacles of the beautiful church in the Temple are regarded by
scholars and antiquarians as such relics—" perfectly intelligible
to the poetic mind of the Hindu," remarks Bonwick, " yet conveying no thought to the Londoner, who would be shocked
enough if the primitive symbol had been retained.   Our love of

* Bonchurch.

what is old, our reverence for what our fathers used, makes us keep still in the church, and on the very altar cloths, symbols which would excite the smile of an Oriental, and lead him to wonder why we send missionaries to his land while cherishing his faith in ours."

In allusion to Egypt and this phallic worship, Herodotus says : " To Bacchus, on the eve of his feast, every Egyptian sacrifices a hog before the door of his house, which is then given back to the swineherd by whom it was furnished, and by him carried away. In other respects the festival is celebrated almost exactly as Bacchic festivals are in Greece, excepting that the Egyptians have no choral dances."

He further says that in celebrating these orgies they fabricated certain obscene images, a cubit in height, so artificially contrived with nerves, that the pudenda, equal in magnitude to the rest of the body, might be moved at pleasure, and these images the women carried about in procession, singing all the time the praises of Bacchus, and dancing to the sound of the flute. He adds that it was Melampus who first introduced among the Greeks the sacrifices in honour of Bacchus, the pomp of the phallus, and all the other ceremonies of that Egyptian superstition.

Aristotle traces the origin of comedy to the ribaldry and the improvised jokes customary at these festivals.

In ancient Rome, Greece, and certain parts of Italy, phallism assumed the form of the worship of Priapus. There was a town of Mysia, on the Propontis, of this name, whose origin was somewhat obscure ; according to some it being a colony of Miletus, while others regarded it as a settlement of Cysicus—anyhow, it derived its name from its worship of the god Priapus.

Priapus is also a term sometimes applied to the genital parts of men, viz., the penis and testes. The name took its rise from Priapus, a fabulous deity particularly adored at Lampsacus, the place of his birth, who for the extraordinary size of his parts was exceedingly revered by the women. From the scriptures and profane history we learn that Maachah, the queen and mother of Asa, had made and consecrated a grove to Priapus, at whose sacrifices she presided. In I. Kings, 15, and II. Chronicles, 14, we are informed that Asa dethroned his mother for this, destroyed and burnt the idols, and cut down the groves.

The Roman poets appear to have held very light notions about this god, and did not scruple to heap upon him both ridicule and abuse. Horace's Eighth Satire, Book I., is an imaginary complaint of Priapus about the incantations of sorceresses. It opens with :— " Formerly I was the trunk of a wild fig-tree, an useless log, when the artificer, in doubt whether he should make a stool or a Priapus of me, determined that I should be a god."

Priapus, among the Romans, was the god of the gardens and orchards, in which they placed his statues. Horace continues :— " Henceforward I became a god, the greatest terror of thieves and birds : for my right hand restrains thieves, and a bloody-looking pole stretched out from my frightful middle : but a reed fixed upon the crown of my head terrifies the mischievous birds, and hinders them from settling in these new gardens."

Priapus is supposed by some to have been the same as Belphegor, the idol of iniquity mentioned by St. Jerome, and his worship is said to have been brought to Lampsacus, whence it passed into Greece and Italy. The mythology of the Greeks and Romans with regard to this god is as follows :—Although authors are not unanimous with regard to his parentage, yet it is most generally allowed that he was the son of Bacchus and Venus. Juno, it is said, being jealous of that goddess, contrived by her enchantments that he should be brought into the world quite monstrous and deformed. On this account Venus removed him out of her sight, and sent him to be educated at Lampsacus. Having afterwards become the dread of husbands, he was banished from that town ; but the inhabitants, afflicted with a secret distemper, recalled him, and from that time he was made the object of public veneration, a temple was built for him, and sacrifices were instituted in his honour. Under this fiction is wrapped up the history of the propagation of the worship of this god from Egypt to Lampsacus, agreeably to an observation sanctioned by the authority of Herodotus, that the birth of a god in any country means only the introduction of his worship in that same country. Accordingly, Priapus was reported to be the son of Bacchus, or Dionysius, who made the conquest of India, and who was the same with Osiris; and Venus, his mother, was the same with Isis. This Egyptian queen, it has been said, had introduced after the death of her husband the infamous ceremony of the phallus.

It has been noticed that, in all probability, it was very late before Priapus was known by either Greeks or Romans, since Hesiod and Homer say nothing of him.

The Abbe Banier affirms that the above is the whole mystery of Priapus, who was represented in the gross obscenities of the worship of the phallus. The excesses committed on the occasion of the feast of this god are far too gross to allow of anything like a minute description, for they were characterised by every species of debauchery, and drunkenness, and lewdness, which could suggest themselves to the inflamed imaginations of the riotous and half-maddened votaries.

Boissart gives a print from a bas-relief which represents the principal feast of Priapus, and shows the wild extravagances indulged in by the infuriated celebrants. It was on such occasions that the heathen publicly rendered adoration and divine honour to those parts of the human body which are not only the lawful organs of generation, but are the instruments of exciting and gratifying the most impure passions. Figures of these were carried about in procession by the women, and hymns of glorification and praise were sung to them. St. Augustine has described these things, for which revelation, says Banier, he had reasons which subsist no more; in only very brief outline, therefore, do we attempt to convey an idea of the true nature of the subject.

The Romans appear to have got their worship of Priapus from the Egyptians, who, under the form of Apis, the sacred bull, worshipped the generative power of nature; and as the syllable *pri* or *pre* signifies, in the Oriental tongue, *principle*, production, or natural or original source, the word Priapus may be translated *principle of production*, or of *fecundation*, *of Apis*. The same symbol bore among the Romans the names of Tutunus, Mutinus, and Fascinum. The latter, signifying a charm against evil influences, explains why it was put over gateways and doors, just as the horse-shoe is by some people in the present day, and hung around the necks of children as a preventative against witchcraft. It was also worn by barren women, in the belief that it would conduce to fruitfulness. For a like purpose votive offerings were often made in the temples, and great numbers of small ones in bronze and porcelain have been found at Pompeii and Herculaneum, and in Egyptian tombs. The Lampsacus previously mentioned seems to have been the most celebrated of the places where the worship of Priapus was practised, chiefly on account of the extreme indecency of the rites. Catullus writes thus:—

> " To thee I dedicate this green retreat,
>   Priapus, sacred be the shade to thee :
> Whether some grove, or Lampsacus, thy seat,
>   Detain thy steps, O sylvan deity!
> Thou who in towns that deck the shelly coast
> Of much-famed Hellespont art worshipp'd most."

The figures of this god varied somewhat in character, though the meaning, of course, was always the same. Ancient pictures and sculptures have come down to us covered with these objects, some of them of the most remarkable nature, but, as we have said, conveying the same intention. One will be seen with the head of a fawn, a human head with the ears and horns of a goat, and another with only a human head and a phallus. A traveller describes one that he had seen in the palace of a cardinal, a statue with a phallus that had served as a sign-post. Priapus would be represented sometimes with a reaping-hook in one hand while his other grasped the organ, which was invariably depicted of an enormous size and displaying intense energy. Women could be seen publicly approaching the god and hanging upon the gigantic phallus garlands, representing their lovers; nay, further, St. Augustine declares that the Roman ladies thought it perfectly decorous, and even pious, for the young brides to seat themselves upon the monstrous and obscene member of Priapus. Lactantius mentions the same thing, explaining it as done in order that the god may appear to have been the first to receive the sacrifice of their modesty; he speaks also of Jutinus, before whom brides sit as an "introduction to the marriage rites," and continues :—" And a thousand other fictions, so that they who regarded these as objects of worship may be said to be more foolish than the Egyptians, who worship certain monstrous and ridiculous images. These, however, have some delineation of form. What shall I say of those who worship a rude and shapeless stone under the name of Terminus?"

And so on, all over the world, the story goes; through Egypt with its Khem and Osiris, India with its Siva, Assyria with its Vul, the Greeks with their Pan and Dionysius, the Teutonic and Scandinavian nations with their Fricco, Spain with its Hortanes, the Phœnicians with their Adonis, and the Phrygians with their Attys. St. Augustine, already quoted, shows that in Rome the worship of the phallus prevailed to such an extent, and with such new attendants and surroundings, and under such new circum-

stances, that it had to be finally suppressed by the authorities.
At the festival of Venus the Roman matrons adored the consecrated emblem in the temple on the Quirinal, and bore it thence
with great pomp to the sanctuary of Venus Erycina outside the
Colline gate, where it was presented to the statue of the goddess
and then returned to the former place. In the spring the Roman
rustics carried the phallus across the fields, to ensure their
fertility. The end of all this was the degeneration of the worship
to the basest level of immorality. It was made to pander to the
filthiest and most licentious tastes of the degraded and vicious,
the end being, as we have said, the compulsory abolition by the
senate in the interests of the state.

Mexico, Central America and Peru were found by the early
invaders not only to have the cross in similar forms to those
used in christian countries, but an abundance of phallic symbols
in addition. In Panuco the phallus was adored in the temples,
and at Tlascala were worshipped both the phallus and the cteis,
and bas-reliefs adorned the public squares, representing, like
those of India, the sexual union.

In Cuzco, in front of the great temple, and in the temples of
Yucatan, stood phallic pillars, and monuments the object of
whose building is lost in antiquity, like the round towers of
Ireland, druidical stones, &c., which are believed by some to
have a similar significance.

Leaden phalli have also been found in the river Rhone, supposed to be the signs and tokens of some secret and licentious
society. The mysterious round towers of Ireland have been
supposed to have the same meaning, and their presence and
nature have been ascribed by some writers to the partial coloni-
sation of the country in remote times by visitors from India,
who erected and dedicated monuments in honour of the regenerative and reproductive powers of nature, under the names of Sol,
Phœbus, Apollo, and Budh.

Very much nearer our own times, and not very far from our own land, however, if certain writers are to be credited, do we find traces of this worship.   One of these says:—"The first bishop of Lyons was honoured throughout Provence, Langue-doc, &c., as a saint, and as his name happened to be Pothin, Photin, or Fotin, commonly pronounced by the lower orders *Foutin*, these people, who are very apt to judge of the nature of things by the sound of the words by which they are designated, thought St. Foutin worthy of replacing St. Priapus, and accord-ingly conferred upon him the prerogatives of his predecessor. Saint Foutin de Varailles had particular reverence paid to him in Provence, nor is this to be wondered at, since the power was attributed to him of rendering barren women fruitful, stimulating flagging husbands, and curing their secret maladies.   It was consequently the custom to lay upon his altar, as was formerly done on that of the god Priapus, small votive offerings made of wax, and representing the weak or otherwise afflicted parts. Sanci says:—' To this saint are offered waxen models of the pudenda of both sexes.   They are strewn in great numbers over the floor of the chapel, and should a gust of wind cause them to rustle against one another, it occasioned a serious interruption to the devotions paid to the saint.   I was very much scandalised when, passing through the town, I found the name of Foutin very common among the men.'   The same saint was similarly honoured at Embrun.   When the Protestants took that town in 1585, they found, among the relics of the principal church, the phallus of St. Foutin.   The devotees of that town, in imitation of pagan ones, made libations to this obscene idol.   They poured wine over the extremity of the phallus, which was dyed red by it.   This wine being afterwards collected and allowed to turn sour, was called holy vinegar, and according to the author from whom this account is taken was applied by women to a most extraordinary purpose; but what that purpose was we are not informed."

It is reported also that the barren women of some of the French villages, not many years ago, used to scrape the wooden phallus of the saint, and mixing the fragments with water, would swallow them, in order to give, as they supposed, efficacy to their prayers that they might be blessed with children.

We have too, in addition, an account of the chapel of St. Guingalais, near Brest, containing a phallus in the form of a wooden beam which passed entirely through the saint's body. Here, as at the former place, the women would rasp its extremity and swallow the dust for a similar purpose. It is said that now and again the indecent symbol would be completely worn away by this process at the point; the priests would then, by a blow at the back, force it forward, so that it appeared miraculously to remain always of one length, notwithstanding the scrapings.

Other French towns also possessed similar emblems, which in the dark ages, under the influence of a corrupt and mercenary priesthood, were equally venerated. A very large phallus, covered with leather and furnished with natural appendages, existed at Orange in the early part of the sixteenth century, but was burnt in the public market place by the Protestants when they destroyed the church of St. Eutropius.

Down to the year 1700, in the Neapolitan Carnival, it was customary to carry in the public processions a wooden statue of Priapus whose private member was so large as to be grossly indecent, reaching as high as the idol's chin. The custom was abolished afterwards by Archbishop Davanzati.

In further illustration of this point we will only add Sir William Hamilton's account of certain proceedings relating to Saints Cosmo and Damianus. " On the 27th of September, at Isernia, one of the most ancient cities of the kingdom of Naples, situated in the province called the Contado di Molise, and adjoining the Aruzzo, an annual fair is held which lasts three days. On one of the days of the fair relics of Saints Cosmo and Damianus are exposed. In the city and at the fair, *ex-votos* of wax, representing the male parts of generation, of various dimensions, sometimes even of the length of a palm, are publicly exposed for sale. There are also waxen vows that represent other parts of the body mixed with them, but of those there are few in comparison of the number of the Priapi.

The distributors of these vows carry a basketful of them in one hand, and hold a plate in the other to receive the money, crying out, " Saints Cosmo and Damianus ! " If you ask the price of one the answer is, "*più ci metti, più meriti*" (the more you give, the more you merit). The vows are chiefly presented by the female sex, and they are seldom such as represent legs, arms, &c., but most commonly the male parts of generation. The person who was at the *fête* in the year 1780, and who gave me this account (the authenticity of which has since been con- firmed to me by the governor of Isernia) told me also that he heard a woman say at the time she presented a vow, " *Santo Cosmo, benedetto, cosi lo voglio* ! " (Blessed St. Cosmo, let it be like this !) The vow is never presented without being accompanied by a piece of money, and is always kissed by the devotee at the moment of presentation."

Of course, as time has gone on, and the priestly hold over the minds of the people has weakened, as men have become refined, enlightened, and educated, this kind of superstition has been on the wane. In the ninth century the use of the phallus as an amulet was so general that it was anathematised by the church, and the anathema was repeated in the thirteenth and fourteenth centuries, but even at the present day in some parts of Italy the peasants still hang the emblem on the necks of their infants, to protect them from the evil eye. Whatever goes on now, however, is as nothing compared with the state of things in former days, when the smiths' forges and the bakers' shops of Pompeii, and

other parts of Europe, bore the emblem in front of them as
a charm to keep away evil and ensure good luck. So numerous
and so universal was the use of such things in ancient times that
Schliemann found them in abundance, at a depth of more than
forty feet, in the *debris* of the supposed Troy.

There is one thing connected with our own English customs,
coming down to almost the present generation, and connected
with this subject, which we would not pass over in silence before
we turn to other parts of the world and the history of more
remote times, viz., the May-day festival, in which the inhabitants
of our villages, and formerly even of London, danced around a
garlanded pole as a sort of welcome to the returning season.

This has often been quoted as a custom purely English, but
most erroneously, as the following will show.   In the *Asiatic
Transactions* a paper by a former Colonel Pearse, dated more
than a hundred years ago, says :—" I beg leave to point out to
the society that the Sunday before last was the festival of Bhavani, which is annually celebrated by the Gopas and all other
Hindus who keep horned cattle for use or profit.   At this feast
they visit gardens, erect a pole in the fields, and adorn it with
pendants and garlands.   The Sunday before last was our first of
May, on which the same rites are performed by the same class of
people in England, where it is well known to be a relique of
ancient superstition in that country ; it should seem, therefore,
that the religion of the East and the old religion of Britain had
a strong affinity.   Bhavani has another festival, but that is not
kept by any one set of Hindus in particular, and this is appro-
priated to one class of people.   This is constantly held on the
ninth of Baisach, which does not always fall on our first of May
as it did this year.   Those members of the society who are
acquainted with the rules which regulate the festivals may be
able to give better information concerning this point, I only

mean to point out the resemblance of the rites performed here and in England, but must leave abler hands to investigate the matter further, if it should be thought deserving of the trouble. I find that the festival which I have mentioned is one of the most ancient among the Hindus."

And in the olden time this May-pole was far more than many an English villager of modern times supposed. It was nothing less than a great phallic emblem, the symbol of the Lord of Life, around which the people rejoiced at the approaching summer, and worshipped the regenerative powers of beneficent Nature.

CHAPTER III.

*Phallic Worship of the East— Linga described— Caves of Ele-
phanta—Lucian and the Temple at Hicrapolis—Small Linga
—Ceremony of Linga-puja—Woman at Worship described—
Hindu desire for children— The Temple of Nuptials— Re-
proach attached to Barren Women—Story of Shravana and
Dasaratha—The Twelve Lingas—Distinction between Linga
and Yoni—Argha—Veneration for Stones—Story of polluted
Brahmins—The Brachmans and Fire production—Feuds be-
tween the Linga and Yoni Worshippers—Legend of Sati and
Parvati.*

IN no country on the face of the earth has phallic worship
prevailed so extensively, and for so long a period, as India.
Our Queen is said to rule there over at least a hundred millions
of pure phallic worshippers, that is, above three times the population of these islands ; hence, it is almost impossible to traverse
any part of the country without coming upon the sometimes
disgusting and repulsive emblems of this peculiar form of
devotion. In a paper read before the Anthropological Society
some twenty-five years ago, by E. Sellon, Esq., it was stated that
" it might be affirmed that there is scarcely a temple in India
which has not its Lingam, and that in numerous instances this
symbol is the only form under which the deity of the sanctuary
is worshipped."

This lingam worship is the Indian form of phallism, and there
is sufficient resemblance in the forms, ceremonies, and symbols of
both to identify them as one and the same. The authority
already quoted says :— " The Linga is a smooth, round, black
stone, apparently rising out of another stone, formed like an
elongated saucer, though in reality sculptured from one block of

basalt. The outline of the latter, which calls to mind a Jew's harp (the conventional form of the *pudendum muliebre*), they term Argha or Yoni. The former (a rounded perpendicular stone), the type of the virile organ, is the Linga. The entire image, to which the name Lingioni is given, is also generally called Lingam."

This symbol of the regenerative power, or representation of the union of the sexes, which it really is, typifying the divine *sacti*, or active energy in union, the procreative generative power seen throughout nature), however, to which great veneration is paid, and to which much mysticism is attached, is made of numerous other materials besides stone—as metals, wood, clay, &c., and is of all manner of sizes, from a few inches to many feet. They are seen sometimes of enormous extent, in the caves of Elephanta, for instance, marking unequivocally that the symbol in question is at any rate as ancient as that temple, as they are of the same rock as the temple itself; both, as well as the floor, roof, pillars, pilasters, and its numerous sculptured figures, having been once one undistinguished mass of granite, which, excavated, chiselled, and polished, produced the fine cavern and forms that are still contemplated with so much surprise and admiration. The magnitude of the cones, too, further precludes the idea of subsequent introduction, and together with gigantic statues of Siva and his consort, more frequent and colossal than those of any other deity, necessarily, as before noticed, coeval with the excavation, indicate his paramount adoration and the antiquity of his sect. A paper in the *Proceedings of the Anthropological Society* states that many of the linga found in the temples are forty feet in height and twenty-five in circumference.

A further instance of the great size of some of these objects may be seen in Dryden's *Lucian*, describing the temple at

Hierapolis and its symbols:—" The two great phalli standing in the porch with the inscription on them, ' These Phalli I, Bacchus, dedicated to my stepmother Juno.' The Greeks erect phalli to Bacchus which are little men made out of wood *bene nasatos*, and these are called *neurospasta*. There is also on the right hand of the temple of a little brazen man, whose symbol is enormously disproportioned. There is also in the temple the figure of a female who is dressed in man's clothes. The priests are self-mutilated men, and they wear women's garments. The temple itself stands upon a hill, in the middle of a city (Hierapolis, the holy city near Aleppo), and it is surrounded by a double wall. The porch of the temple fronteth the north, and it is two hundred yards in circumference; within it are the two phalli before mentioned, each about a hundred and eighty feet high. To the top of one of these phallic pillars a man ascends twice during the year, and he remains there seven days at a time. The vulgar imagine that he converseth with the gods above and prayeth for the prosperity of all Syria, which prayers the gods hear, near at hand. He never sleeps during the seven days. Within the temple's precincts were kept oxen, horses, eagles, bears, and lions; they are in no way noxious to men, but may be handled freely."

" A curious manner of testifying his respect to a stepmother," says the comment by Wieland and others in Tooke's version. " Yet it should not be forgot that this foundation was apparently instituted at a time when the reverence of the fair sex for this powerful and venerable talisman was not only immensely great, but likewise frankly and unblushingly avowed and manifested. Besides, nothing can be more futile than this hypothesis of making Bacchus, the son of Semele, the builder of the temple at Hierapolis, and nothing shallower than the arguments which the Græculi (with whom Lucian here perhaps only seems out of irony to coincide) urge in its behalf. To all appearance these phalli were without comparison older than the inscription, and had reference to the primitive religions of that country, which acknowledged only two aboriginal deities, Heaven and Earth, the Uranoo and Ge of the Greeks : that is, the spirit, or the vivifying principle of heaven, which by its energy and influence fructifies the earth, and renders it the mother of all things. The former, in those rude, and in some sense innocent ages, typified under the symbol here spoken of ; and accordingly the religious veneration for the phallus, which indicated, not the sexual sign abstractedly, but referred to the thereby creative or generative principle, and universal father, and which certainly in the early ages nobody thought harm of."

Lucian further states in reference to this climbing " Others believe it has reference to Deucalion, and is done in remembrance of that horrible inundation which to escape men climbed the highest hills and mountains. This does not appear probable to me, and I think that it is done purely in honour of Bacchus. I conclude so from hence; whoever raises phalli to Bacchus, uniformly places little wooden men upon them : to what end anybody else may tell. I therefore think that the living man goes up merely to represent the wooden.

The manner of climbing is this :—the priest winds a long rope about himself and the phallus, then sets his feet on a sort of wooden peg which is driven into the phallus, projecting exactly so far as to serve for a foothold by bearing against it with the tips of his toes ; and thus he swarms and shoves himself up little by little, at the same time raising the rope on both sides in proportion as he ascends, with the motion of a coachman who slackens the rein as the horses urge their speed. He that has never witnessed this practice may form an idea of it if he has heard how, in Arabia and Egypt and other parts, they climb the palm trees. When he is at the top he lets down another long and strong cord that he has with him, and draws up by it wood, clothes, vessels, and whatever materials he likes, to make a sort of nest with, wherein he sits, and, as I said, must remain seven days, during which time numbers of the devout come and bring gold and silver (some perhaps let copper coin suffice), and laying their oblations down on the ground, at the bottom of the phallus, tell their names and go away. Another priest, standing near, reports the name of each to him above, who says his prayers for every one by name, which he accompanies upon a kind of metallic instrument that gives a very loud and shrill sound. During all this time he never sleeps a wink. But enough of these phallus climbers."

Linga are seen also of diminutive size, for domestic adoration or for personal use, some individuals always carrying one about with them; and in some Brahmin families one is, or was, daily constructed in clay, placed, after due sanctification by appropriate ceremonies and prayers, in the domestic shrine, or under a tree or shrub sacred to Siva, and honoured by the adoration of the females of the household.

There is a temple to every village, and in each temple lingas are found, generally two or three feet in height, and rising conically from a broadened base. In early morning the girls who are desirous of obtaining lovers and husbands flock to these temples for acts of adoration—for the ceremony called " Linga-puja," in which they first sprinkle the god with water from the Ganges, the linga is then decorated with garlands of the tulva flower, followed by gesticulation with the fingers, and the recitation of the prescribed form of incantation, after which they rub themselves against the emblem and pray the deity to make them fruitful in child-bearing.

In Moor's *Hindu Pantheon* there are a large number of plates illustrating this subject more fully, which the reader is advised to inspect, should he desire to get a clear and definite idea of it.

These plates are engravings of genuine Hindu pictures, and may
be confidently regarded as faithful representations of the originals,
as such giving a far better notion of the nature of the different
objects than could be attained by any amount of verbal description.   Plate 22 is particularly worthy of notice, as it represents
a young and beautiful woman in the act of performing the
ceremony called Linga-puja.   The domestic temple in which the
symbol is placed is called, as temples generally are, " Dewal," or
" Deval," from *Dcva*, a deity, and *havela*, a house; literally, a
house of God.   The building, in English, is called a Pagoda.
The lingha and argha are of black stone with gilt edges.   The
linga (the upright conical stone), which has mystical orange-
coloured lines traced on it, is crowned with encircled folds of
bilva flowers ; and a chaplet of three strings of them, white, with
yellow buds at regular distances, hangs pendant from the top of
the linga, falling towards the termination or spout of the argha.
(The bilva is a shrub consecrated to Mahadeva, who alone wears
a chaplet of its flowers, which are offered in sacrifice to no other
deity).   Five lamps (*pancharty*) are used in puja to Siva, sometimes one lamp with five wicks ; the rest of the furniture consists
of a spouted vessel (*jari*) to hold lustral water brought from the
Ganges, for sprinkling the god ; a cup (*dipa*) for ghee (clarified
butter) for feeding the lamps ; another cup (*novady*) for water
with which to sprinkle the flowers and linga ; and a bell (*gaut'ha*)
which is rung at certain times to scare away evil spirits.

In the picture the young woman is seated upon an embroidered
carpet, holding a rosary of 108 beads in her hand, her attention
abstractedly fixed upon the deity. She is represented propitiating
Mahadeva in his generative character, indicated by the linga
inserted in its appropriate receptacle, the argha or yoni (*i.e.*, the
male generative organ inserted in that of the female).   She may
be imagined as invoking the deities, typified by their symbols,
for the blessing of fruitfulness ; its reverse being deprecated by
both sexes as the most afflicting visitation of divine displeasure.

As the Hindoos depend on their children for performing those ceremonies to their manes which they believe tend to mitigate punishment in a future state, they worship linga to obtain fecundity.   Husbands whose wives are barren send them to worship linga at the temples, and it is said that the wives take pretty good care that their errand shall be productive of the desired effect.

The Temple of Nuptials contains two distinct apartments, one considerably larger than the other, having recesses in each.   This room is ascended by four steps; from the veranda it is the first in rotation.   The outer veranda, or gallery, is dissimilar to most of those divisional front apartments in the other temples : here it is divided from the back apartment by a wall, having regular apertures for doors, and windows for the admission of light.   It is different from most of the other verandas in being nearly as large as the inner room.   The length of this veranda is sixty-four feet six inches, it is eight feet broad and twelve feet high ; whilst the room is only sixty-seven feet long and nineteen feet eight inches broad ; it is not, however, so high by a foot.   There are three small recesses in this room, two of which are six feet square, and six feet high ; the third recess is exactly one foot larger in the square than the others.

A few yards from this veranda and hall is another excavation, having the same appellation as the previous one.   This is a larger and finer temple than its neighbour, containing a room twenty-one feet square, placed in a spacious recess, forty feet six inches in depth and thirty-eight feet broad.   Its square room contains a ling of Maha-Dev.   Outside of the door are colossal figures, similar to those in Dhurma Linga, but only in the front square ; they represent Chand and Prichand.   The figures that are grouped with them were called by different names to those that accompany the same figures in Dhurma Linga, and are proportionably small in stature, but are exceedingly well executed.

The chief ornaments, however, in this apartment, are two handsome and singularly-shaped pillars, and two pilasters that adorn the entrance of the recess, which give a very pleasing effect to the square temple standing behind, showing itself between the intervals of the pillars. The length of the hall (exclusive of the recess) is one hundred and eleven feet by twenty-two feet six inches. After passing the outer part, the room is contracted by the recess, in which stands the temple and the scarf; this part is enriched with several figures with drapery round their middle. The Brahmins, as usual, had names for them, but they were generally known as servants of Kama. A traveller says :—" My Brahmin cut all discussion short by affirming, with a supercilious smile, they were ' *Kunchnce Luq*,' in other words, ' *Dames des plaisirs*.' *

No symbol is more venerated, or more frequently met with in all parts, than the altar and ling of Siva, or Maha-Dev. Barren women constantly resort to it to supplicate for children. The efficacy of their prayers, and the mysteries attending them, we have already dwelt upon. Sterility in a female in India is the greatest possible human misfortune. A wife may be formally repudiated on that score, nor is this the only misfortune ; the young people scoff at her, her own sex avoid her, and her husband upbraids her. In short, it is supposed to be a curse inflicted by the gods. There is a striking allusion to this in the first chapter of St. Luke's Gospel, where it is said :—" After those days Elizabeth conceived, and hid herself five months, saying, Thus hath the Lord dealt with me in the days wherein he looked on me, to take away my reproach among men."

" The Lingham," says a traveller, " in the small temple was covered with oil and red ochre, and flowers were daily strewed on its circular top. This emblem is much frequented by female

* Seeley.

votaries, who take especial care to keep it clean-washed, and
often perfume it with odoriferous oils and flowers, whilst the
attendant Brahmins sweep the apartment, and attend the five
oil lights and the bell-ringing."

In illustration of this subject we have a story in Moor's *Hindu
Pantheon*, which in substance runs thus :—Dasaratha had three
wives, but was childless, and after many fruitless acts of piety, &c.,
betook himself, almost in despair, to the jungles or forests —
that is, to a life of abstinence and devotion. It happened that a
Brahmin, named Shravana, was at this time resorting with his
aged and infirm parents to a *jatra*, or holy fair ; and the old
people being faint with thirst Shravana went in search of water
to a *baluri*, near to which Dasaratha had taken his secret stand,
expecting game. Hearing the gurgling of the water in Shravana's vessel he let fly his arrow, and hastening to his supposed
game, discovered his unhappy error, and that he had wounded a
Brahmin. This he lamented deeply, but was consoled by the
forgiving Shravana, who desired that he might be left to die.
Dasaratha made known their son's fate to the unhappy parents,
who imprecated, in prophetic agony, a fate like his on the
wretched homicide. Miserable in thus having destroyed a
Brahmin and his parents, who sank under their affliction, super-
added to his constant sorrow of being childless, Dasaratha did
not deprecate the fate they threatened, but declared that could
he once behold the face of a son, now, from the sensations excited
by the recent scene, more than ever desired, he could die
contented. Distracted by his trying situation, he repaired for
advice and consolation to a learned Guru, named Vasishtha, who
directed him how to perform the funeral rites, and what sacrifices were necessary to be made in expiation of the enormous sin
of slaying a Brahmin. All was done, with due extent of
charitable distribution, and he was further desired to take from

the remains of the *homa* a portion of certain articles, such as rice, ghee, sugar, &c., and to make them into three cakes or balls; and, with pious devotion, repairing home, to give, after certain ceremonies, one cake to each of his three wives. He did so: one to Kahunsilya, one to Kaosalya, and the other to Kahikeya; but the latter, knowing herself to be the youngest and favourite wife, was very much put out that she had not been the first complimented by her lord on his return, and looking disdainfully on it as she held it in her hand, a kite made a swoop and carried it off. Grievously afflicted at this, and apprehensive that, the ceremonies being incomplete, her chance of pregnancy was thereby forfeited, she gave way to grief and lamentation, which moved her two kind sharers in their lord's benevolence to give her each half of their better guarded cakes; and those respective proportions were accordingly, with due anxiety and hope, severally eaten, and with due effect, for they soon all proved to be with child.

Returning to the vanished cake, it is related that a married Brahmany, named Anjeni, being childless, had piously performed divers acts leading to fecundity, such as supplication and sacrifice to Mahadeva, daily prayers and offerings to linga, &c., &c., and had by these powerful means so extorted the favour of the generative deity, Rudra, that he promised her an incomparable offspring, and directed her to fix her eyes in profound attention on the sun, holding upwards the palms of her hands (in the posture of suppliant expectancy), and to eat directly any substance that might, heaven directed, fall therein, calling on his name. The cake that the kite had borne off from Kahikeya fell in, and she ate it as ordered, and became pregnant, and in due season was delivered of a son, of such surpassing prowess that at his birth he ground to powder a large stone that happened to be near. This child was Hanuman.

It is noticeable that like as it was in the dark ages, when the superstitious flocked to certain shrines with offerings, and made painful pilgrimages to them, so has it been with the Hindoos, who had their favourite shrines of the lingam. " Twelve Lingas are mentioned in the *Kedara Kalpa* of the *Nahdi-upa-Purana* as being of transcendent sanctity. In this *Purana* Siva is made to say :—' I am omnipresent, but I am especially in twelve forms and places.' Then follows a list of the twelve localities alluded to, one of which, Ramasa, at Letabundha, on the island of Ramissarum, between Ceylon and the continent (where the Linga is reported to have been set up by the god Ram, or Ramā) has one of the most splendid of all the Indian temples, with a magnificent gateway a hundred feet in height. In each of these temples the only image of Siva or Mahadev that attracted devotees was a Lingam. From this circumstance there can be little doubt that the religion of the Saivas is nothing more than a gross system of phallic idolatry." *

The mention of lingam worship reminds us of the necessity of pointing out more clearly the distinctiveness of two things which are often confounded. It has been said, writers on this subject, generally, perhaps unavoidably, commix their speculations on the linga and yoni. Crude nature is personified and called Prakriti ; she is declared to be nature, or the earth, the womb of nature ; she is thence anything concerning or containing, or the power or *sacti,* of such faculties. In its first state that power was rather a tendency, an aptitude, and lay dormant until excited by the *bija,* or vivifying principle, the *aura* of nature, personified in Siva, who in this character is called Parusha, or the primeval male. Here we find nature passive and active : the power or aptitude of nature is symbolised by the yoni, the vivifying principle by the linga. Prakriti is found to be one of the names and forms of Parvati, as Parusha is of Siva.

* Sellon.

The faculty or power of containing, of which the Yoni is the type, is also called Argha by Hindoo mystics. The name is given to a cup, or dish, or vessel, in which fruits and flowers are offered in oblation. These vessels, they say, ought always to be boat-shaped; and so they frequently are, but sometimes round, oval, or square—mostly, however, circular. The rim of the Argha is more especially the Yoni, while the contents of the vessel represent the Linga, which is sometimes more unequivocally figured by an image of Siva standing erect in the centre of the Argha. Hence, one of his names is Arghanatha, or lord of the boat-shaped vessel.

The Argha as a type of the *power of conception*, excited and vivified by the Linga or Phallus, Mr. Wilford † supposes to be one and the same with the ship Argo, which, according to Orpheus, was built by Juno and Pallas, or, according to Apollonius, by Pallas and Argus, at the instance of Juno. The word Yoni, as it is usually pronounced, nearly resembles the name of the principal Etruscan goddess; and the Sanscrit phrase, *Arghanatha Iswara,* seems accurately rendered by Plutarch, when he asserts that Osiris was commander of the Argo. That the Sanscrit words *p'hala*, meaning fruit, and *p'hulla*, a flower, had ever the sense of *phallus* is not affirmed; but as these are the chief oblations in the Argha, and are confessed to be a representation of the Linga, their sounds may easily have been so transferred. We have seen, too, that Mahadeva himself, the prototype of the Linga, is some times placed erect in the Argha (several plates in Seely's *Temples of Elora* distinctly show this, and will at once be recognised as the male and female organs united): this is to complete a mystical tri-union of powers; for Vishnu, the principle of humidity and of conservation, is symbolised by a convexity or embossment in the centre of the Argha, over which the image of Mahadeva, or the *p'hala* and *p'hulla*, as representing the Linga, or Phallus, are

† *Asiatic Researches,* 3.

placed. The idea that the Sanscrit *p'hala* or *p'hulla* may in sense, as well as sound, be cognate with and the source of the Greek *phallus*, derives strength from the fact that Mahadeva, in his character corresponding with that of Jupiter Marina, or Neptune, bears, like his Roman kinsman, a trident, called *Triphula* and sometimes *Triphala*, denoting trifurcation and triflorescence. Jupiter Triphylus is thus identified with the three-eyed Siva.

We have seen that the vessel bearing the name Argha is boat-shaped, and a type of the world. In the general deluge the generative powers of nature, male and female, reduced to their simplest elements, the Linga and Yoni, assumed this shape for the preservation of mankind. Brahma, the creative power, is represented to have been asleep at the bottom of the abyss; this alludes to the destruction of mankind, man being represented in the abstract by Brahma. The Yoni becoming boat-shaped, the Linga was the mast, and protected by Vishnu rode upon the waters. It seems that everything hollow or concave, having the property of containing, reminds mystics of Argha or Yoni, as aspiring objects do of the Linga. Enthusiasts see these two principles; that is, they say, nature passive and active, dormant and revivified, everywhere and in everything,—the earth, the sea, a boat, a well, a pond, the hollow of the hand, clefts in rocks, excavations, caves, partake of relationship with the one,— mountains, especially if insulated and conical, pyramids, cones of any sort, fire, a mast, a tree, obelisks, &c.,— all these connect themselves with ideas of Mahadeva and the Linga. The earth is typified by a boat; the Argha of the Hindoos, and the Cimbium of the Egyptians. Osiris is represented in a boat carried by men:—in India, Mahadeva erect in the Argha refers to the same allegory. All over India the Argha, and Linga of stone inserted in it, is found an object of worship.

Seely says :—" To this very day, in India, I have observed on
the roadside, where a murder has been committed, a rude stone,
with the figure of a horseman with a drawn sword; or, for
robbery, a camel or bullock, having a pack on his back. Large
heaps of stones are often seen by the roadside, on which are
placed flags of a dirty brickdust colour. To each of these heaps
every pious traveller adds a stone as he passes, till the heap
becomes a little mound. If any of these is at all like the Linga
of Mahadeva, it is sure to be selected, placed conspicuously
upright, daubed with oil and red ochre, the peculiar colour of
Brahma. This veneration for stones we find mention of in the
Scriptures, Genesis 28, v. 18 :—' And Jacob rose up early in the
morning, and took the stone that he had put for his pillow, and
set it up for a pillar, and poured oil upon the top of it.' "

Caves we have noticed as types of the Yoni, from their property
of hollowness, of containing, and also from the shape of their
mouth. The most ancient oracle and place of worship at Delphos
was that of the Earth, in a cave, which was called Delphi; an
obsolete Greek word, synonymous with Yoni in Sanscrit, it being
the opinion of devout Hindoos that caves are the symbol of the
sacred Yoni. This opinion prevailed also in the West, for per-
forations and clefts in stones and rocks were called *Cunni
Diaboli* by the first Christians, who always bestowed the appellation of devils on the deities of the heathen. Perforated stones
are not uncommon in India, and devout people pass through
them, when the opening will admit of it, in order to be regenerated. If the hole be too small, they put either the hand or the
foot through it, and with a sufficient degree of faith it answers
nearly the same purpose. One of the seven wonders of the Peak,
in Derbyshire, is called the " Devil's Cavern," but very im-
properly, for this wonderful cave, or at least one very much like
it in the Sacred Isles, and particularly noticed in the *Puranas*, is
declared to be the sacred Yoni. The cleft called Guhya-sthan, in

Nepal, answers fully and literally to the coarse appellation bestowed upon the other in Derbyshire by the vulgar, and is most devoutly worshipped by numerous pilgrims from all parts of India.*

Adoration of stones is found similarly spread through the superstitious ages of all nations. The Hindoos retain it with undiminished bigotry, and will affirm, and indeed go nigh to prove, that such objects, from the sacred monolithic subject of the Kaaba, at Mecca, or the obelisks of Egypt, to the trilithic temple at Stonehenge, with many intermediate, are no other than their Linga under various forms and denominations. Clefts in rocks, rent by the hand of nature, may therefore be supposed to be profoundly venerated by such enthusiasts as are Hindoo mystics. One of the most celebrated in India (already noticed in these pages) is at the promontory on the island of Bombay, called in English, Malabar point. The promontory itself, thrusting its apex into the sea, which thus forms a *sandya*, or junction, is lingaic. In former times it was much resorted to, and its sin-expelling potency much relied on, before its purity and privacy were polluted and interrupted by the presence of strangers, and the increasing population of the island. The density of its present population, and the extending prevalence of foreign manners, have lessened the sanctity of this spot, now the constant resort and abode of persons who look on the local superstitions with an eye too rational or curious to encourage their continuance. †

The passing of the diseased through clefts in the rock in various places, has been curiously improved upon by the early priests of India. They had rich sinners to deal with, as well as poor ones, and while the cleft in the rock did very well for the latter, something more costly was designed to meet the case of

---

* Wilford.—*Asiatic Researches*, Vol. 6.   † Rees.

the former ; so in certain cases of defilement, it was required that an image of pure gold should be made of the female power of nature, either in the form of a woman or of a cow ; in this statue, the person to be regenerated was enclosed, and obtruded through the usual channel.

In Moor's *Hindu Pantheon* and the *Asiatic Researches*, Vol. 6, we have recorded an interesting incident which will fairly illustrate this. There are four rivers, which were once much dreaded by religious people. It was forbidden even to touch the waters of the Carmanasa, to bathe in the Caratoya, to swim in the Gandaci, and to cross the Indus. When the unfortunate Raghu-Nath-Raya, or Ragoba, sent two Brahmins as ambassadors to England, they went by sea as far as Suez, but they came back by the way of Persia, and of course crossed the Indus. On their return, though men of irreproachable life, they were treated as outcasts, because they conceived it hardly possible for them to travel through countries inhabited by impure tribes, and live according to the rules laid down in their sacred books ; it was also alleged that they had crossed the Attaca. Numerous meetings were held in consequence of this and learned Brahmins were convened from all parts. The influence and authority of Raghu-Nath-Raya could not save his ambassadors. However, the holy assembly decreed, that in consideration of their universal good character, and of the motive of their travelling to distant countries, which was solely to promote the good of their country, they might be regenerated and have the sacerdotal ordination renewed. For the purpose of regeneration it was directed to make an image of pure gold of the female power of nature in the shape either of a woman or of a cow. In this statue, the person to be regenerated was enclosed and dragged out through the usual channel. As a statue of pure gold and of proper dimensions would be too expensive, it was sufficient to make an image of the sacred Yoni, through which the person to be regenerated was to pass.

E

Raghu-Nath-Raya had one made of pure gold and of proper dimensions : his ambassadors were regenerated, and the usual ceremonies of ordination having been performed, and immense presents bestowed on the Brahmins, they were readmitted into the communion of the faithful.

Another illustration of the extraordinary prevalence of phallic worship in India is supplied by the method used by the Brachmans for producing fire. Those who devote themselves to the priesthood were required to kindle fire always by the process of attrition. This was done on their entering the sacerdotal office by means of a piece of apparatus called *arani*, constructed and used as follows :—A piece of wooden plank, a foot long and six inches in diameter, had a small conical hole, a socket, in the upper side, into which was introduced the end of a pin, about a foot long and an inch in diameter, the other end of which formed a moveable handle ; this was held steady in the left hand of the operator, who with a bow, having its string twice wound loosely round the upright pin, twirled it quickly backwards and forwards with his right hand. The pin and socket fitting closely, the attrition of the two pieces of hard wood soon produced fire. The flat piece of wood was usually laid on the ground or floor, previously purified by a plastering of cow-dung and appropriate prayers, &c., and steadied by the foot of the operator, as well as by the pressure of the upright pin. Every officiating Brachman, it was said, ought to possess one of those machines, with which to light the fire for his own funeral pile, as well as for his nuptial ceremonies and the obsequies of departed ancestors, and for the performance of solemn sacrifices.

Fire being so curiously, and to the ignorant so wonderfully produced by the operation of the *arani*, that instrument and the process, as well as the product, are objects of admiration and superstition. Siva as well as Pavaka, being one personification of fire, and a cone being its type, as the form naturally assumed by ascending flame, that figure was also a type of Siva. The pin of the *arani* terminated in a cone; but an inverted cone was a symbol of Vishnu, who, as well as fire, was also a personification of water, which, in its natural property of descent, assumes the shape of an inverted cone. Thus this part of the *arani* reminded the mystic of Siva, as well from the form of its termination, as from its erect position; and also of Vishnu from the position of its cone; but principally of Siva, whose peculiar emblem the linga, or phallus, was thus doubly exhibited in both form and position; while the other part of the *arani*, the hollow conical receptacle, was no less striking to such visionaries, as the figure of the sacred Yoni, the most mysterious of forms, the symbol of the Sakti, or consort of the generative Siva.

It is a remarkable thing that in this singular kind of worship feuds prevailed between Hindoo sects, as bitter as any that have agitated the world in later times. There were two parties, the Lingacitas and the Yonijas, the former worshipping the Linga and the latter the Yoni, and these were at such variance as to which was the superior in the production of a perfect offspring, that frequent and terrible wars broke out between them. In Vol. 3 of the *Asiatic Researches* Mr. Wilford says:—" This diversity of opinion seems to have occasioned the general war, which is often mentioned in the *Puranas*, and was celebrated by the poets of the West as the basis of the Grecian Mythology, I mean that between the Gods, led by Jupiter, and the Giants, or Sons of the Earth, or in other words between the followers of Iswara and the Yonijas, or men produced, as they asserted, by Prithivi, a power or form of Vishnu, for Nonnus expressly declares that the war in question arose between the partisans of Jupiter and those who acknowledged no other deities but Water and Earth; according to both Nonnus and the Hindoo mythologists, it began in India, whence it was spread over the whole globe, and all mankind appear to have borne a part in it.

These religions and physiological contests were disguised in
Egypt and India under a veil of the wildest allegories and
emblems.   On the banks of the Nile Osiris was torn in pieces,
and on those of the Ganges the limbs of his consort, Isi or Sati,
were scattered over the world, giving names to the places where
they fell, and where they still are superstitiously worshipped.
In the book entitled *Maha cala sanhita* we find the Grecian story
concerning the wanderings of Damater, and the lamentations of
Bacchus; for Iswara, having been mutilated through the imprecations of some offended Munis, rambled over the whole earth,
bewailing his misfortune, while Isi wandered also through the
world, singing mournful ditties in a state of distraction.   There
is a legend in the Servanasa of which the figurative meaning is
more obvious.   When Sati, after the close of her existence as
the daughter of Dacsha, sprang again to life in the character of
Parvati, or Mountain-born, she was re-united in marriage to
Mahadeva.   This divine pair had once a dispute on the comparative influence of the sexes in producing animated beings, and
each resolved, by mutual agreement, to create apart a new race
of men.   The race produced by Mahadeva was very numerous,
and devoted itself exclusively to the worship of the male deity;
but their intellects were dull, their bodies feeble, their limbs
distorted, and their complexions of many different hues.   Parvati
had at the same time created a multitude of human beings, who
adored the female only, and were all well-shaped, with sweet
aspects and fine complexions.   A furious contest ensued between
the two races, and the Lingajas were defeated in battle; but
Mahadeva, enraged against the Yonijas, would have destroyed
them with the fire of his eye if Parvati had not interposed and
appeased him; but he would spare them only on condition that
they should instantly leave the country, with a promise to see it
no more; and from the Yoni, which they adored as the sole cause
of their existence, they were named Yavanas.

It is evident that this strange tale was invented to establish the opinion of the Yonijancitas, or votaries of Parvati or the Yoni, that the good shape, strength and courage of animals depend on the superior influence of the female parent, whose powers are only excited and put into action by the male *aura*. But the Lingacitas maintain an opposite doctrine. There is also a sect of Hindoos, by far the most numerous of any, who, attempting to reconcile the two systems, tell us in their allegorical style that Parvati and Mahadeva found their concurrence essential to the perfection of their offspring, and that Vishnu, at the request of the goddess, effected a reconciliation between them; hence, the navel of Vishnu, by which they mean the *os tincæ.* is worshipped as one and the same with the sacred Yoni.

CHAPTER IV.

Legend concerning Mahadeva —Diodorus Siculus on Osiris— Ptolemy Philadelphus —The Vaishnavas —Hindoo Sects — Worship of the Female Generative Principle —The Fakirs and the Hindoo Women —Hold of Phallism on the Hindoo mind—Origin of Phallic Worship in India—Hindoo Prayer.

MANY curious legends are extant concerning Linga, Yoni, Arghi, &c., such as the following, for instance :—One day as Mahadeva was rambling over the earth, naked, and with a large club in his hand, he chanced to pass near the spot where several Munis were performing their devotions. Mahadeva laughed at them, insulted them in the most provoking and indecent terms, and lest his expressions should not be forcible enough, he accompanied the whole with significant signs and gestures. The offended Munis cursed him, and the Linga or Phallus fell to the ground. Mahadeva, in this state of mutilation, travelled over the world, bewailing his misfortune. His consort, too, hearing of this accident, gave herself up to grief, and ran after him in a state of distraction, repeating mournful songs. This is what the Greek mythologists called the wanderings of Damater and the lamentations of Bacchus.

The world being thus deprived of its vivifying principle, generation and vegetation were at a stand, gods and men were alarmed; but having discovered the cause of it they all went in search of the sacred Linga, and at last found it grown to an immense size, and endowed with life and motion.

Having worshipped the sacred pledge, they cut it into thirty-one pieces, which polypus-like, each became a perfect Linga. The devotees left one-and-twenty of them on earth, carried nine to heaven, and one to the inferior regions, for the benefit of the inhabitants of the three worlds. To satisfy Devi, and restore all things to their former situation, Mahadeva was born again in the character of Baleswara, or Iswara, the infant, but suddenly became a man, under the title of Lileswara, or Iswara ("who gives delight,") and after various adventures met his consort, then in the character of Sami Rama (the Semiramis of the Greeks) who, by the sweetness of her voice in chanting her own metamorphosis and that of Lileswara, attracted the notice of her former and future spouse in his present character, till now entirely indifferent to the female sex. The goddess soon became Lileswari, and was happily re-united to her lord.*

The Hindoos insist that the black stone in the wall of the Kaaba is no other than the Linga or Phallus of Mahadeva, and that when the Kaaba was rebuilt by Mohammed, as they affirm it to have been, it was placed in the wall out of contempt; but the newly converted pilgrims would not give up the worship of the black stone, and the ministers of the new religion were forced to connive at it.

With respect to the monstrous origin of Balesa (Baleswara) and the thirty-one Phalli, it was suspected by the Hindoo astronomers to be an attempt to reconcile the course of the moon to that of the sun, by dividing the synodical revolution into thirty-one parts, which may represent also three hundred and ten years. To the event related is ascribed the origin of the Linga or Phallus, and of its worship; it is said to have happened on the banks of the Euphrates, and the first Phallus, under the name of Baleswara Linga, was erected on its banks. This is confirmed by Diodorus Siculus, who says that Semiramis brought an obelisk from the mountains of Armenia, and erected it in the most conspicuous part of Babylon. It was 150 feet high, and is

* *Asiatic Researches*, 4.

reckoned by the same author as one of the seven wonders of the world. The Jews, in their Talmud, allude to something of this kind : speaking of the different sorts of earth of which the body of Adam was formed, they say that the earth which composed his generative parts was brought from Babylonia.*

From Diodorus Siculus we learn that Osiris after travelling about all over the world, and becoming by his discoveries the benefactor of mankind, died, and that the manner of his death was kept secret by the priests in their own registers, but that after a time it became noised abroad that he had been murdered by his wicked brother Typhon, who mangled his dead body into six-and-twenty pieces, giving a piece to each of his confederates, so as to bring the same guilt equally upon them all. But Isis with the assistance of her son Orus, revenged his death upon Typhon and his accomplices, and possessed herself of the kingdom. She also made diligent search for the parts of her husband's body, which she found, all but his privy members. She then fastened the pieces together, cementing the whole with wax and spices, and bringing them to a figure about the size of Osiris, committed it to the care of the priests, at the same time instituting the mystic rites of Isis and Osiris, in honour of her murdered husband. She then bound them over to keep her secret, giving them ample reward for their services, and whenever the rites were celebrated, a similar search was made for the missing parts. These however had been thrown by Typhon into the Nile, because none of his partners would receive them, yet they were divinely honoured by Isis, for she commanded an image (*aidoion*) of this very part to be set up in the temples and to be religiously adored ; and in all their ceremonies and sacrifices to this god, she ordered that part to be held in divine veneration and honour. The Greeks, therefore, after they had learned the rites and cere-

† *Asiatic Researches*, 3.

monies of the feasts of Bacchus, and the Orgian solemnities from the Egyptians, in all their mysteries and sacrifices to this god, adored that member by the name of Phallus. By the order of Isis, figures of the male organs were constructed, and fixed to poles, and were thus carried about during the festival.

Athenæus informs us that Ptolemy Philadelphus, at one of those magnificent festivals, displayed to the Egyptians a Phallus of gold, richly painted and adorned with golden crowns, a hundred and twenty cubits in length, with a star of burnished gold upon the top, the circumference of which was six cubits. This was borne aloft, like the other idols, on a splendid car, and, like them, received homage from the gazing crowd.

The Vaishnavas, in order to appropriate the creative principle to Vishnu, make Brahma, whom they acknowledge as the immediate agent of creation, to derive his origin from a Lotos, which sprang out of the navel of Vishnu, whilst sleeping upon the vast abyss of primeval waters; thus Vishnu becomes superior to Brahma, as being the cause, first, of his existence, and secondly, of all created things through his agency. The Argha is a vessel of copper used by the Brahmins in their puja; its shape is intended to represent the universal Mother, but in the centre of it is an oval rising embossed, and by this, the Vaishnavas assert, is meant the navel of Vishnu, from which all things originally sprang; and by the mystic union of these two principles of production it is intended to describe them as identically one. The Saivas, however, insist that this omphalic rising is meant as the emblem of the Linga; hence Siva's title of Arghanatha, and in the Agama, Argha-Isa—both meaning the Lord of the sacred vessel Argha.

Vishnu is represented in the tenth Avatar as the destroying power, thus ascribing to him the attribute of Siva.

Vishnu is represented by the Vaishnavas with four arms, and in each hand he bears a symbol. These symbols seem intended to unite the three great attributes in him, and to express his universal supremacy. The *Lotos* typifies his creative power (in allusion to the lotos which sprang from his navel). The *Sauc'ha* typifies his attributes of preservation, and the mace that of destruction; while the *Chacra* expresses his universal supremacy (as *Chacra-Varti*, or Lord of the Chacra); when applied to a monarch it indicates universal empire; applied to a pundit, the possession of the whole circle of science.

When the personified attributes of the Deity ceased to be considered as mere hieroglyphics; when mankind began to view them in the light of distinct persons, and, attaching themselves to the worship of one or of the other exclusively, arranged themselves into sects, the worshippers of Siva introduced the doctrine of the eternity of matter. In order to reconcile the apparent contradiction of assigning the attribute of creation to the principle of destruction, they asserted that the dissolution and destruction of bodies was not real with respect to matter, which was indestructible itself, although its modifications were in a constant succession of mutation; that the power which continually operates these changes must necessarily unite in itself the attributes of creation and apparent destruction : that this power and matter are two distinct and co-existent principles in nature; the one agent, the other patient ; the one *male*, the other *female* ; and that creation was the effect of the mystic union of these principles.

The hieroglyphic of this union was worshipped under a variety of names—Bhava and Bhavani, Mahadeva and Maha Maya, &c. Thus the attribute of creation was usurped from Brahma by the followers of Siva, to adorn and characterise their favourite deity.

This seems to have been a popular worship for a great length of time. Two sects, however, sprang up out of it. The one personified the whole universe, and the dispensations of Providence in the regulation thereof, with a goddess. This sect retained the female symbol only, and denominated themselves Sacta, as worshippers of the *Sacti*, or female power, exclusively. which they call *Pracriti*, and which we from the Latin term nature.

The other sect insisted that there was but one eternal first cause; that everything existing derived its existence from the sole energy of that first cause.

In order, therefore, to express their ideas of the absolute independence of this supreme power upon any extra co-operation, they took for their symbol the male emblem, unconnected with the female.

A third sect likewise arose, which intended to reconcile the idea of the unity of godhead with that of the existence of matter and spirit; they therefore contended that the union of those two principles was so mysteriously intimate as to form but one being, which they represented by a figure half male and half female, and denominated Hara-Gauri, and Ardhanari-Is-Wara. It is probable that the idea of obscenity was not originally attached to these symbols, and it is likely that the inventors themselves might not have foreseen the disorders which this worship would occasion amongst mankind. Profligacy eagerly embraces what flatters its propensities, and ignorance follows blindly wherever example excites; it is therefore no wonder that a general corruption of manners should ensue, increasing in proportion as the distance of time involved the original meaning of the symbol in darkness and oblivion. Obscene mirth became the principal feature of the popular superstition, and was, even in after times, extended to and intermingled with gloomy rites and bloody sacrifices, a heterogeneous mixture, which appears totally irreconcilable, unless by tracing the steps which led to it. It will appear that the engrafting of a new symbol upon the old superstition occasioned this strange medley. The sect of Vishnu was not wholly free from the propensity of the times to obscene rites;

it had been united in interest with that of Siva, in their league against the sect of Brahma, as was expressed by an image called Har-Heri, half Siva and half Vishnu.   This union seems to have continued till the time when an emblem of an abstract idea, having been erected into an object of worship, introduced a revolution in religion which had a violent and extended effect upon the manners and opinions of mankind.*

"The Vaishnavas are divided into many sects, whose object of worship, though alike pertaining to all, is adored in a more or less gross manner, according to the practice of the particular one to which they belong.   They comprise the Goculasthas, the Yonijas, the Romani, and the Radhaballubhis, an account of some of whose practices it may, perhaps, be interesting to notice.

The Goculasthas adore Krishna, while the Romani worship Ramchunda; both have again branched into three sects,—one consists of the exclusive worshippers of Krishna, and these only are deemed true and orthodox Vaishanas (Krishna being an *avata*, or incarnation of Vishnu).

As Parameswarra, Krishna is Jaganath (or Lord of the Universe), and represented black, the apparent colour of ether, or space.   The Krishna lingas are consequently also of the same colour, those of Siva being white.   The Lingionijas adore Krishna and Radha united (*in coitu*).   The Radhaballubhis dedicate their offerings to Radha only (as the *Sacti* or energy of Vishnu). They worship a naked girl, presenting to her the offerings intended for the goddess; in other words, the girl acts the part of Radha, in the same manner that some young girl may have been selected, to take the part of the Virgin Mary, in the religious plays or mysteries of the Middle Ages.   When these people are travelling, or on a voyage, and a female is not to be obtained for this purpose, their oblations are made to the yoni (*i.e.*, to an image of the

---

* Paterson, in *Asiatic Researches*, Vol. 8.

pudendum muliebre).   Hence they are called also Yonijas, as
being worshippers of the female *Sacti,* or power,—in contradis-
tinction to the Lingayetts, or adorers of phallus.   This naked
worship is peculiar to the Sactas, and appertains to the Tantrica
or black magic.

The worship of the female generative principle, as distinct from
the deity, appears to have originated in the literal interpretation
of the metaphorical language of the Vedhas, in which will, or
purpose to create the universe, is represented as originating from
the Creator, and co-existent with him as his Sacti (or bride), or
part of himself.   The Sama Vedha, speaking of the divine cause
of creation, says, "He experienced no bliss, being isolated,—
alone.   He ardently desired a companion, and immediately the
desire was gratified.   He caused his body to divide, and became
male and female; they united, and human beings were made." *

A remarkable phase of the kind of worship now under consideration, may be seen illustrated in a plate found only in the French
edition, published at Amsterdam in 1728, of Bernard Picart's
Ceremonies et Coutumes Religieuses.   The plate in question exhibits some of the penances and religious customs of that fanatical
and disgusting body of men known as fakirs.   The word fakir is
Arabic and signifies poor, and is applied to a certain class of
religious beggars well known in India, and who have managed
to obtain an extraordinary command over the superstitious pre-
dilections of the people.   These men go about entirely without
clothing, with long hair matted and filthy with dust plentifully
showered upon it in acts of devotion and penance.   By their
extravagant self-inflicted tortures, they have obtained great repute
for holiness of life; they will remain sometimes buried to the
neck in a pit, without food or drink for many days in succession;
they put fire upon their heads until they burn not only the
hair but the entire scalp; they will keep a hand clasped tightly

* Sellon.—*Anthrop. Soc. Mem.*

upon itself till the nails actually grow into the flesh; they will
carry the head thrown backwards for so long a time that they
are unable to restore it to its proper position; they will carry an
arm in one position till it stiffens in its unnatural attitude and
cannot be put down again. Upon approaching a village in the
course of their wanderings, the inhabitants forsake their houses
and go out to meet them, competing with each other for the honour
of the holy men's company. It seems, however, that instead of
being pious and devout men, they are, for the most part, when not
insane, the most filthy and licentious of beings. Great as is their
influence and power over the people generally, it is greater still
over the women, who treat them with the most unreserved famil-
iarity, and who seem to lay aside every shred of modesty in their
intercourse with them; accordingly, in their intense desire to have
children, many of the females visit the fakirs, and offer a kind of
worship to the parts brought into action in the procreation of a
family. They will, without a blush, without the slighest emotion,
without a thought that they are doing anything unbecoming,
kneel in front of the naked and filthy wretch who has come
amongst them, take his private member in their hands, and im-
print upon it a kiss of impassioned fervour. By this worship of
the phallus they hope to win the favour of the gods, and so be
enabled to produce the children, whose absence is almost sure to
lead to ill treatment on the part of their husbands. The extent
of the influence exercised by these men may be inferred from the
estimate in *D'Herbelot's Bibliothèque Orientale,* that there have
been in India at one time, as many as two millions of them,
Mohammedan and Hindu.

The extraordinary hold of phallism upon the Hindoo mind,
and the universal prevalence of its objects of worship, are
certainly unequalled in the case of any other religion known.
On the higher parts and in the centre of the earth the Hindoos
place a mountain standing like a column, 84,000 yojans high,

3,200 broad at the top, and 16,000 at the bottom. It is circular and in the shape of an inverted cone. This idea prevailed once in the West, for when Cleanthes asserted that the earth was in the shape of a cone, this is probably to be understood only of the mountain called *Meru* in India. Anaximenes said that this column was plain, and of stone, exactly like the *Meru-pargwetle* of the inhabitants of Ceylon, according to Mr. Joinville, in the seventh volume of the *Asiatic Researches*. " This mountain," says he, " is entirely of stone, 68,000 yonas high, and 10,000 in circumference, and of the same size from the top to the bottom." The divines of Thibet say it is square, and like an inverted pyramid. Some of the followers of Buddha, in India, insist that it is like a drum with a swell in the middle, like drums in India, and formerly in the west. Leucippus had said the same thing, and the Buddhists in India give that shape also to islands. This figure is given as an emblem of the reunion of the original powers of nature. *Meru* is the sacred and primeval Linga, and the earth beneath is the mysterious Yoni, expanded and open like the padma or lotos. The convexity in the centre is the *os tincæ*, or navel of Vishnu, and they often represent the physiological mysteries of their religion by the emblem of the lotos, when the whole flower signifies both the earth and the two principles of its fecundation. The germ is both *Meru* and the Linga; the petals and filaments are the mountains which encircle *Meru*, and are also the type of the Yoni; the four leaves of the calyx are the four vast regions towards the cardinal points, and the leaves of the plant are the different islands in the ocean round Jambu; and the whole floats upon the waters like a boat. The Hindoos do not say, like the Chaldeans, that the earth has the shape of a boat, which is only the type of it. " It is their opinion, I do not know on what authority," says Mr. Wilford, " that at the time of the flood the two principles of generation assumed the shape of a boat with its mast, in order to preserve mankind.

Enthusiasts among the Hindoos see these two principles everywhere—in the clefts of rocks, commissures of branches, peaks
among mountains, &c. The earth is typified by a boat—the
Argha of the Hindoos, the Cymbium of the Egyptians, which are
also emblems of the earth and of the mysterious Yoni. The Argha
or Cymbium signifies a vessel, cup, or dish, in which fruits and
flowers are offered to the deities, and ought to be in the shape of
a boat, though we see many that are oval, circular, or square.
Iswara is called Arghanatha (the lord of the boat-shaped vessel),
and Osiris, according to Plutarch, was commander of the Argo,
and was represented by the Egyptians in a boat carried on the
shoulders of a great many men, who, I think, might be called
with propriety Argonauts. The ship worshipped by the Suevi,
according to Tacitus, was the Argha, or Argo, and the type of
the mysterious Yoni. The Argha with the Linga, of stone, is
found all over India as an object of worship. It is strewed with
flowers and water is poured on the Linga. The rim represents
the Yoni and the *fossa navicularis*, and instead of the Linga
Iswara might be represented standing in the middle, as they used
to do in Egypt." *

To these instances given by Mr. Wilford, says Moore, of
mystical types arising from contemplating any ordinary aber-
ration of nature in the mind of an enthusiastic Hindoo, may be
added a fancied mystery in any regular excavation. If he dig a
pond the Hindoo, if a Saiva, imagines it a type of the Yoni, or
Devi, and cannot fully enjoy the comforts it offers him until it be
reunited to the other types of elemental nature. The water that
this Argha or Yoni encloses is a symbol of Vishnu, who is in
physics a personification of humidity in general; here it is his
navel. After numerous ceremonies, expensive according to the
means of the party, a mast is, on a lucky and sacred day, inserted

* *Asiatic Researches*, 8.

into the centre of the mysterious Yoni, or tank; the mast represents the Linga, or Siva, and now the typical reunion of the original powers of nature is complete. The last ceremony of placing the Linga, or mast, is commonly called the marriage of the Linga and Yoni; strictly speaking the brim of the tank is the Yoni, its area the Argha. In front of most temples of eminence is seen a tank (some of them exceedingly beautiful), and in the centre of the tank a mast, generally with wooden steps nailed up its sides, in order to reach the Linga, or mast, to decorate it with flowers, sprinkle it with water, or place lights on it.

" In the opinion of those who compiled the Puranas, the phallus was first publicly adored by the name of the *Basê-warra Linga* on the banks of the *Cumu-daoti* or Euphrates.

The supposed founder of the worship (as we learn from the *Halakanara MS.* in *Mackenzie's Collections*), was Baswa Basava, or Baswapa, the son of Madijah Rajah, a Brahmin, who with his wife, Madevi, inhabited the town or district of Hin-guleswur-parbuttee-agaharam, on the west side of Sri Saila, and both devout votaries of Mahadeo, or Siva. From an inscription on the great Singaleswarra Linga (one of the twelve), and also on one at Keneri, carved *in relievo* in the rock commemorative of the event, it appears that, in approval of this Puja, the great god and goddess manifested themselves to those devoted followers by springing, in a miraculous manner from the before mentioned emblem, while the Brahmin and his spouse were in the act of devotion; and we behold in this relievo these persons in a kneeling posture, recessed at the base of the Lingam.

But it is not only the votaries of Siva who adore their god under the symbolic form of Phallus. The Viashnawas (or followers of Vishnu) use the same medium. They also are Lingayets — one of the essential characteristics of which is wearing the Linga on some part of their persons. It is either of silver, copper, gold, or beryl; the fascinum of the Romans, and the jettatura of modern Italy." *

* Sellon.—*Anthrop. Soc. Mem.*

F

" The gods said, ' O Lord what means ought we to adopt? '
Brahma replied ' Propitiate by adoration the mountain born goddess, and she will then assume the form of the Yoni and receive
this Lingam, by which means alone it can be rendered innocuous.
Should you thus obtain her favourable assistance, then form a
vessel of the eight kinds of leaves, place in it boiled rice and
sacred plants, and having filled it with holy water consecrate the
whole with the proper prayers and invocations, and with this
water, repeating at the same time suitable prayers, sprinkle the
Lingam.   After also Parvati shall have, under the form of the
Yoni, received the Lingam, do you erect and consecrate the form
of the Lingam in the Yoni (Linioni), and by adoring it with
offerings of flowers, perfumes, and such things, and by kindling
lamps before it, and by singing and music, propitiate Maheshwa
and thus will the forgiveness and favour of that god be undoubtedly obtained.'   Having heard these words, the gods and sages
hastened to implore the protection of Siva, and the assistance
of Parvati, as directed by Brahma; and these deities having been
propitiated, Parvati, under the form of the Yoni, received the
Lingam, and thus appeased its consuming fire, and in commemor-
ation of this event was instituted the worship of Lingam." †

† *Shiva Puran*, Part I.—*Linga-vidhanam.*

CHAPTER V.

Indian and Egyptian Worship compared —Hindoo Soldiers in Egypt—Bruhm Atma, the Breathing Soul—Growth of Hindoo Religion—Worship of Siva—Benares—The Lingayets—Character of Hindoo Emblems and Ornaments—Favourable View of Hindoo Emblems—Charge of Indecency against Hindooism.

SOME eighty years ago a writer in the *Edinburgh Review* pointed out certain points of comparison between the Osiris of Egypt, the Bacchus of Greece, and the Siva of India, in the folowing terms :—" Osiris was adored in Egypt, and Bacchus in Greece, under the emblem of the Phallus. It is under the same emblem that he is still venerated in Hindoostan, and Phallus is one of his names in the dictionary of Amara Singha. The bull was sacred to him in Egypt. Plutarch assures us that several nations of Greece depict Bacchus with a bull's head, and that when he is invoked by the women of Elis they pray him to hasten to their relief on the feet of a bull. In India he is often seen mounted on a bull, hence one of his Sanscrit names, Vrishadwaja, signifying, " whose ensign is a bull."

The Ganges, in like manner, is fabled by the Hindoos to flow from the tresses of Siva; hence another of his names, Gangadhara, " the supporter of the Ganges." We conceive, by the way, that Scaliger and Selden are mistaken in supposing that Siris, the Egyptian name of the Nile, is synonymous with Osiris. Siris seems to us the Sanscrit word *saras*, a river in general, or *the* river, from its imputed superiority. Isis is the consort of Osiris, Isa that of Iswara, or Siva. The attributes of the goddesses might be shown to correspond as precisely as those of their lords.

The attendants of Iswara resemble in their frantic demeanour the furious Bacchants of the god of Naxos. It is remarkable that many of the appellations by which the Greeks distinguish Bacchus are also used by the Hindoos; but instead of applying them to Baghesa himself, the latter gave them to his son, whilst both nations have their legends to account for them. Thus the Greeks named Bacchus Dimeter, "having two mothers"; the Hindoos call Skanda, the son of Baghesa, Divimati, with the same signification. Pyrignes, "born from fire," and its equivalent in Sanscrit, Agnija, are respectively Greek and Indian appellations of Bacchus and Skanda. The title of Thrianbus, we are told by Diodorus, was assumed by the Greek deity in his triumph after the conquest of India. Tryambo, in like manner, is one of the most common appellations of the Indian Bacchus, but we are not aware of its signification.

A circumstance occurred some years ago which illustrates in a remarkable manner the similarity of Pagan systems which we have been alluding to, and as it is too well authenticated to admit of doubt it is of particular value. It was this:—During the expedition into Egypt against the French, the Indian soldiers, who had been taken there by the Red Sea and Suez to assist in the work, recognised many of the mythological forms, especially the bull and some stone figures of serpents, as similar to what they had in their own country. They at once made this known to their officers, affirming that the people who formerly inhabited Egypt must have been Hindoos; and when they saw the temple at Hadja Silsili in a state of decay they were filled with indignation that the natives should have allowed it to fall into such a condition, as they conceived it to be the temple of their own god, Siva.

Again and again we have pointed out the difficulty of ascertaining the origin of the worship of the native people of India. It is fairly buried in antiquity, and though the various theories set up and explanations offered are interesting, it cannot be said that they are in any special degree reliable. That they were originally worshippers of one god only is the opinion of the best of scholars, and the tradition from which this is derived says this deity was designated Bruhm Atma, the "Breathing Soul." The early simplicity of Hindoo worship, with its comparatively few ceremonies, in the course of time became greatly changed, and their god was represented in a somewhat grossly physical form by a rough pillar of stone, called by them the Linga, which was nothing else than the Phallus. This was their representation of the procreative or regenerative power in nature, and it is almost impossible to exaggerate the profundity of the reverence in which it was held, and which was rendered to it in worship. They supposed that all the beneficent operations of nature were owing to its influence — the birth of men and animals, the growth and ripening of the seeds and crops, the formation and perfection of the richest fruits—all were due to this image.—Such was the idolatry of the Hindoo in his earliest and simplest times; it afterwards gradually assumed a more complicated character. Then what they called the Elements, a heathen Trinity, were evolved from Bruhm, bearing the names of Brahma, Vishnu, and Siva (Creator, Preserver or Saviour, and Destroyer). "On these," says Sellon, "were conferred three *gunas,* or qualities, viz., *Rajas* (passion), *Sat* (purity), and *Tumas* (darkness). This is the *Trimurti.*

Soon after this we have the institution of Avatas and Avantaras, the greater and lesser incarnations, by which one or other of the triad imparted a portion of his divine essence both to men and to brutes. And then speedily came the installation of innumerable gods, by the deification of all the known heavenly bodies, of the elements, of the attributes of the Supreme Being, of those of the Evil Spirit, until at last nearly a million gods were created. Of all these none received such honour as Siva.

" As the Destroyer, and one who revels in cruelty and bloodshed, this terrible deity, who has not inaptly been compared to the Moloch of Scripture, of all their divinities suggests most our ideas of the devil. It may therefore be concluded that the most exalted notion of worship among the Hindoos is a service of fear. The Brahmins say that the other gods are good and benevolent, and will not hurt their creatures, but that Siva is powerful and cruel, and that it is necessary to appease him." *

Siva is sometimes found depicted in the ordinary human form, but this is not that in which he is usually adored. It is generally as the Linga that he is found, as we have described it—a smooth stone rising out of another stone of finer texture ; *simulacrum membri virilis, et pudendum Muliebre.*

The worship of Siva under the type of Linga is almost the only form in which that deity is reverenced, and it is generally regarded as the most ancient object of homage adopted in India, subsequently to the ritual of the Vedas, which was chiefly if not wholly addressed to the so-called elements, and particularly to fire. How far the worship of the Linga is authorised by the Vedas is doubtful, but it is the main purport of several of the *Puranas.* There can be no doubt of its universality at the period of the Mohammedan invasion of India. The idol destroyed by Mahmud of Ghizni was nothing more than a Linga, being, according to Mirkond, a block of stone of four or five cubits long and proportionate thickness. It was, in fact, one of the twelve great Lingas then set up in various parts of India, several of which, besides Somesvara, or Somnath, which was the name of the Siva demolished by Mahmud, were destroyed by the early Mohamedan conquerors. Most, if not all of them, also, are named in works of which the date cannot be much later than the eighth or ninth century, and it is therefore to be inferred, with

* Sellon.—*Annotations.*

as much certainty as anything short of positive testimony can afford, that the worship of Siva, under this type, prevailed throughout India at least as early as the fifth or sixth century of the Christian era. Considered as one great branch of the universal public worship, its prevalence, no doubt, dates much earlier, but the particular modifications under which the several types received their local designations, and became entitled to reverence, are not in every case of remote antiquity." *

Benares appears to have been the principal locality in which this form of worship prevailed, and there were forty-seven Lingas (the principal deity Siva under the name Viweswarra, being one) of pre-eminent sanctity ; there were, however, hundreds of others of an inferior character worshipped, while thousands once famous had fallen into oblivion. Nearly all the chief objects of pilgrimage in this place were similar blocks of stone, and it has been remarked as a singular fact, that " upon this adoration of the procreative and sexual *Sacti* (or power) seen through nature, hinges the whole gist of Hindu faith, and notwithstanding all that has been said by half-informed persons, to the contrary, this puja does not appear to be prejudicial to the morals of the people."

There is a form of Linga worship which it may be well just to mention here, as its name sometimes appears and may cause enquiry. It is that of the Lingayets, Lingawants, or Jangamas, and the distinguishing feature of this is wearing the emblem on some part of the dress or person. This is small in size and made of copper or silver, and is usually hung about the neck or fastened to the turban. The worshippers known under the names mentioned, like the Sapas generally, smear their foreheads with Vibhuti or ashes and wear necklaces and rosaries made of the Rudraksha seed. The priests wear garments of a red colour, generally stained with red ochre. There are very few of these

* Wilford, in *Asiatic Researches.*

however in Upper India, and they are not often met with; when
they are seen it is generally as beggars leading about a bull, the
living type of Nandi, the bull of Siva, decorated with housings of
different colours, and strings of cowrie shells; the conductor
carries a bell in his hand, and travels about the country supported
by the gifts of the people.   In the southern parts of India, the
Lingayets are very numerous, the Saiva priests being generally of
this sect, and are called Aradhya and Pandaram.

The learned Baboo Rajendralala Mitra, in his *Antiquities of
Orissa* says:—"In describing the merits of Orissian Art I must
not forget to notice the despicable taste which the artists have
displayed by making some of their figures most disgustingly
obscene.   By this I do not refer to their nudity, for, as justly
observed by Professor Lübke, the task of sculpture is to conceive
man in his full natural beauty.   Hence the nude figure in its
strictest sense is required.   The perfect harmony and beauty of
the whole can only be displayed in the unclothed form."   This
canon has been more or less accepted by artists and men of taste
in every age and clime, and the Urijas have rather evinced a true
sense of the proper sphere of sculpture by chiselling the nude, and
not thereby given offence to good taste.   But they have added
thereto certain licentious representations which do not admit of
description, their number is small, and they by no means enter
into the general scheme of ornamentation of the temples; but
there they are; and their existence cannot but offer a violent
shock to all modern sense of propriety and decency.   I enquired
of many learned pundits at Puri, as to why such offensive figures
had been allowed to desecrate the sanctuary of the Divinity; but
they could tell me nothing worth hearing.   In one instance obscenity in a temple has been accounted for on the supposition of
its being expiatory.   In a note on Kajraha, with reference to
Rashibuddin's mention of that town, Sir Henry Eliot states, that
" in the *Pithviraj Rayasa* mention is made of a Brahmin woman,

Ilemavani by name, who committed a little *faux pas* with the moon in human shape, and, as a self-imposed punishment for her indiscretion, held a *Banda jag*, a part of which ceremony consists in sculpturing indecent representations on the walls of temples, and holding up one's foibles to the disgust and ridicule of the world." The story occurs in the first Canto of the Benares MS. of Chand and in Mr. Growse's translation of it mention is made of the Bhandava sacrifice, but without any allusion to indecent representations on temples, and I can nowhere find a description of the ceremony in any Sanskrit work. Possibly there may be some authority for it, and the obscenity on Hemavati's temple at Kharjinpur or Kajraha might be accounted for, on the supposition that she wished to expiate her fault by a disgusting public confession. But it is scarcely to be supposed, that all the principal sculptured temples of Orissa owe their indecent ornaments to a like cause, and I am disposed to think that the explanation is more ingenious than true. It is much more probable that the indecent figures on the old Central Indian temples were due to the same cause which produced them in Orissa. What that cause was, it is difficult now to say with perfect certainty. A vitiated taste aided by general prevalence of immorality might at first sight appear to be the most likely one ; but I cannot believe that libidinousness, however depraved, would ever think of selecting fanes dedicated to the worship of God, as the most appropriate for its manifestation ; for it is worthy of remark that they occur almost exclusively on temples and their attached porches, and never on enclosing walls, gateways, and other non-religious structures. " Our ideas of propriety " according to Voltaire, " lead us to suppose that a ceremony " (like the worship of Priapus), " which appears to us so infamous, could only be invented by licentiousness ; but it is impossible to believe that depravity of manners would ever have led among any people to the establishment of religious ceremonies. It is probable, on the contrary, that this custom was first introduced in times of simplicity,—that the first thought was to honour the deity in the symbol of life which it has given us; such a ceremony may have excited licentiousness among youths, and have appeared ridiculous to men of education in more refined, more corrupt, and more enlightened times, but it never had its origin in such feelings. Besides, vicious propensities have, in India, been everywhere and at all times most emphatically denounced, and there is no creed known in this country which does not condemn it as hateful. It is out of the question, therefore, to suppose that a general prevalence of vice would of itself, without the authority of priests and scriptures, suffice to lead to the defilement of holy temples. A religious sanction for it must be sought, and this, I believe, occurs in the fact of most of the temples, on which the offensive figures are shown, being dedicated to the mystical adoration of the phallic emblem. From a very early period in the history of religion, the phallic element has held a prominent place in the mind of man. Most of the leading religions of the ancient world—the Egyptian, the Chaldean, the Assyrian, and the Mosaic, manifested it in some form or other; and in primitive unsophisticated states of society, philosophical conceptions of the mystery of generation had not yet given to the various parts and members of the human body those names which constitute the special vocabulary of obscenity of the present day, many symbols and representations were not only held inoffensive but sacred, and their presence on ancient monuments, therefore, cannot be a matter of surprise."

Quoting various instances of the exhibition and adoration of the Phallus, the Baboo proceeds :—" These and many other instances which could be easily multiplied, were it worth while, suggest the conclusion that the public exhibition of the Phallus in the early ages, had nothing in it which partook of indecency. All ideas connected with it were of a reverential kind. Thousands upon thousands of Hindu men, women and children, visit the Orissian temples every year ; they undertake long tedious journeys in the most inclement of Indian seasons ; undergo the greatest privations, to have a sight of them ; and return home with the firmest conviction, that they have by the pilgrimage freed themselves of all their sins, without even indulging in the nearest shadow of an idea that there is anything improper or indecorous in all that they have seen. The whole to them is a mystery—a mystery of ancient times hallowed by age, and enveloped in everything that is pure and holy,—and none attempts to lift the veil, or pry into secrets, or their causes, which his ancestors for centuries left untouched. You may point out the offensive character of the representations before him, and create a cloud of anxiety and uneasiness in his mind, but it is only a passing cloud, that soon melts away before the fervour of his faith."

"It is some comparative negative praise to the Hindus, that the emblems under which they exhibit the elements and operations of nature, are not externally indecorous. Unlike the abominable realities of Egypt and Greece, we see the Phallic emblem in the Hindu Pantheon without offence ; and know not, until the information be extorted, that we are contemplating a symbol whose prototype is indelicate." Pictures, it is said, " may be turned and examined, over and over, and the uninformed observer will not be aware, that in several of them, he has viewed the typical representation of the generative organs or powers of humanity. The external decency of the symbols, and the difficulty with which their recondite allusions are discovered, both offer evidence favourable to the natural delicacy of the Hindu character." " I am not, however," says Moor in his *Hindu Panthcon*, prepared to deny the appearance, in many instances, of strong evidence to the contrary : the disgusting faithfulness of natural delineations, and the combinations so degrading to human nature, observable on some of the temples and sacred equipages of the Hindus, are deeply offensive to common delicacy and decency.

Blavatsky the author of *Isis Unveiled*, speaking of the occurrence of Phallic emblems in Christian lands, says :—" We find it rather unwise on the part of Catholic writers to pour out their vials of wrath in such sentences as these : ' In a multitude of pagodas, the phallic stone, ever and always assuming, like the Grecian *batylos*, the brutally indecent form of the *lingham* . . . the Maha Deva.' Before casting slurs on a symbol, whose profound metaphysical meaning is too much for the modern champions of that religion of sensualism *par excellence*, Roman Catholicism, to grasp, they are in duty bound to destroy their oldest churches and change the forms of the cupolas of their temples. The Mahody of Elephanta, the Round Tower of Bhangulpore, the minarets of Islam — either rounded or pointed — are the originals of the *Campanilo* column of San Marco, at Venice, of the Rochester Cathedral, and the modern Duomo of Milan. All of these steeples, turrets, domes, and Christian temples, are the reproductions of the primitive idea of the *lithos*, the upright phallus." " The western tower of St. Paul's Cathedral, London," says the author of the *Rosicrucians*, " is one of the double *lithoi* placed always in front of every temple, Christian as well as heathen." Moreover, in all Christian churches, particularly in Protestant churches, where they figure most conspicuously, the two tables of stone of the Mosaic Dispensation are placed over the altar, side by side, as a united stone, the tops of which are rounded. The right stone is the *masculine*, the left *feminine*. Therefore neither Catholics nor Protestants have a right to talk of the indecent forms of heathen monuments, so long as they ornament their own churches with the symbols of the Lingham, and Yoni, and even write the laws of their God upon them."

Much of this will, no doubt, strike our readers as not only extravagant but absurd, especially the forced and unnatural meaning given to the two tablets found in English churches, inscribed with the laws of the ten commandments. It is well known to most people, that those tables contain respectively man's duty to God and to his neighbour, and that it is only by a wide and wild stretch of imagination, they can be made to represent the masculine and the feminine; the statement, however, is given to show the extraordinary lengths to which men have gone in endeavouring to recognise the phallic everywhere in Christian or Pagan ornamentation.

CHAPTER VI.

CROSSES IN GENERAL, AND THE CRUX-ANSATA.

ABOUT few things, perhaps, of a religious character, have
more erroneous notions prevailed, than the symbol of the
Cross. This ornament, of every possible description, carved in
wood and stone or worked in various kinds of metals, precious or
base, meets us everywhere in the world, either as an adornment
to the person or as a conspicuous feature in ecclesiastical archi-
tecture, and there is a pretty general impression afloat that it is
of Christian origin and belongs exclusively to that religion.
Nothing, however, could be more fallacious, and nothing more
calculated to impart wrong ideas of religious history, for the world
abounds in monuments of a cruciform character, which existed
ages before the first proclamation of Christian doctrine anywhere.

Of course, as various writers have observed, the distinction
between the Cross and the crucifix must be duly noted, or even
this statement will be misapprehended; the crucifix—the Cross
bearing the image of a dead man—is Christian exclusively, but
the Cross, pure and simple, though adopted and used by Christians

as a memorial of the instrument by which their founder was put to death, or as an emblem of their faith, dates back to very early times indeed, and is common upon Pagan monuments everywhere. Contemporaneous with the appearance of anything like formal and systematic Pagan beliefs, no symbol, whatever it might mean, was more common or sacred. In other places, we remark upon the similarity of heathen creeds and practices, whether in the far away East or extreme West, whether the worshipper has been Japanese, Hindoo, Egyptian, Greek or Briton, and in each and all alike, the cross has been found the one symbol common to all. It has been described as the aboriginal possession of every people of antiquity, the elastic girdle so to say, which embraced the most widely separated heathen communities ; the most significant token of a universal brotherhood, the principal point of contact in every system of Pagan mythology.

' That mighty maze, but not without a plan,' to which all the families of mankind were severally and irresistibly drawn, and by which their common descent was emphatically expressed, or by means of which each and all preserved amid every vicissitude of fortune, a knowledge of the primeval happiness and dignity of their species." *

Not from written history, in the ordinary acceptation of the term, so much, has this knowledge been derived, but from the comparatively imperishable relics of peoples who have long since passed into oblivion. Ages have rolled away into nothingness, as it were, and the strifes of the world have been fought out, and civilisation with its giant strides has sped along, revolutionising society, and manners, and men, amidst the ever-standing monuments of antiquity, or the silence of the desert plain, broken only by the wild bird's cry or the crash of the tempest, and has reigned over the grave of the fallen greatness of cities mightier than any

* Edin. Rev. 1870.

now to be met with; but the tomb of the dead monarch, the
mysterious mound whose interior generation after generation had
looked upon but failed to explore, the wrappings of the mummy
five thousand years embalmed, the ruins of ancient temples and
palaces, statues, coins, vases, domestic implements, coffins, tumuli,
sepulchral galleries, have made history, if at first difficult to
unravel, at any rate unchangeable and reliable when once understood, and the Cross has been found in and upon all, entering
into the composition of the simplest as well as the most gorgeous
and beautiful of ornaments and structures. There was a sacredness about it, whatever might be the occasion or circumstances
which gave rise to its use, that led to the most extraordinary
expenditure of labour, skill, and wealth in its production. The
ambitious cravings of the worshippers were responded to by toil-
some work almost incredible in its magnificence and extent, and
by the exercise of the profoundest ingenuity of which the human
mind was capable. "Populations of essentially different culture,
castes, and pursuits, vied with each other in their superstitious
adoration of it and in their efforts to extend the knowledge of its
exceptional import and virtue amongst their latest posterities."
Let the wonders of Elephanta and Ellora—their tremendous
rock-hewn caves unequalled for weird grandeur by anything else
owned by the world — let the great temples of Mathura and
Terputty of the East, let the marvels of Calleruish and New-
grange in the West, and the temple at Mitzla (the City of the
Moon) in Central America, hewn, as those of India, from the
solid mountain, the works of peoples intellectually and geo-
graphically distinct, and followers of independent and unassociated
deities, bear witness to the one endeavour to magnify and per-
petuate the same grand primeval symbol. Never was there such
a symbol for universal adoption and adoration; sacred emblems
there were in abundance, belonging to this or that nation or
tribe, but the Cross was international, and we are acquainted

with none, whether that of St. Andrew or St. George, Maltese, Greek, or Latin, but it existed in the remotest ages of antiquity, and can be actually looked upon in the painted or sculptured form. Strangely enough, the passing ages have brought no change worth mentioning in its form. Dynasties, empires, races, cities, have risen, and flourished, and fallen, the barbaric has developed into the splendid and refined, and the simple and unadorned has become the ornate and the beautiful, but these Crosses have survived the shocks of all changes, and the very thing which the sculptor of ancient Babylon and Nineveh carved upon his statues, or the ancient Egyptian painted upon the coffin or mummy-cloth of his sacred dead, as a symbol of his Paganism, is fashioned by the modern builder in stone, or by the jeweller in precious stones and gold, for the Christian temple and the orna-mentation of the Gentile lady's person.

Such is the truth concerning this extraordinary symbol, and it would be no advantage to the Christian religion, to which it has been supposed exclusively to belong, to deny or attempt to con-ceal it. Nothing is gained or lost by any party, by full and complete statements in accordance with ascertained facts, and in these pages we shall do our best to supply truthful accounts of all that has been discovered bearing upon the subject. "For my own part," says the Rev. Baring Gould, "I see no difficulty in believing that it formed a portion of the primæval religion, traces of which exist over the whole world among every people, that trust in the Cross was a part of the ancient faith which taught men to believe in a Trinity, in a War in Heaven, a Paradise from which men fell, a Flood, and a Babel; a faith which was deeply impressed with a conviction that a Virgin should conceive and bear a Son, that the Dragon's head should be bruised, and that through shedding of blood should come Remission. The use of the Cross as a symbol of life and regeneration through water is as widely spread over the world as the belief in the ark of

G

Noah. May be, the shadow of the Cross was cast further back into the night of ages, and fell on a wider range of country than we are aware of.

It is more than a coincidence that Osiris by the Cross should give life eternal to the Spirits of the Just; that with the Cross Thor should smite the head of the Great Serpent, and bring to life those who were slain; that beneath the Cross the Muysca mothers should lay their babes, trusting by that sign to secure them from the power of evil spirits; that with that symbol to protect them the ancient people of Northern Italy should lay them down in the dust." *

Turning for a moment from the extreme East to the West of the world, we meet with the fact that when the Spaniards invaded America they were overwhelmed with surprise to find the sign of the Cross in common use by men considered in every respect to be heathens; yet there was what they deemed only a Christian emblem, and availing themselves of the opportunity thereby afforded of ingratiating themselves with the natives, they showed it emblazoned upon their standards and obtained a reception far more cordial than they had any reason to expect. So great was the veneration of these people for the sign, that it had become more to them than the " Life " of Egypt or the " Eternity " of India; in short it had been set up as an idol and treated with divine honours.

It has been declared by travellers and explorers to be exceedingly difficult sometimes to distinguish between the ancient Crosses and those set up by the invaders; there are many, however, still standing, of too great an age to belong to the designs of that people. With other signs and ornaments, similar to those of Europe, Egypt, India, and China, they are found amongst the extensive ruins of the cities, carved upon the altars

* *Ancient Myths.*

and walls of the temples. Mr. Stephens, in his work on Central America, bears witness to this, and gives a representation of one of the finest he had come across. It was found carved upon the wall of the ruined temple at Palenque and was about nine or ten feet in height. On either side was a human figure, one of them holding up a child as if he were offering it to the old Cross; each of these men had crosses on their vestments.

Stephens says:—" This tablet of the Cross has given rise to more learned speculations than perhaps any others found at Palenque. Dupaix and his commentators, assuming for the building a very remote antiquity, or at least, a period long antecedent to the Christian era, account for the appearance of the Cross by, the argument that it was known and had a symbolical meaning among ancient nations long before it was established as the emblem of the Christian faith."

One of the most remarkable Crosses of the Mexicans was one made by the priests at the festivals, of maize and the blood of the victims offered in the sacrifices. After being worshipped, this image was broken up and distributed to the people who devoured it as a bond of union and brotherhood.

The city of the Moon has already been mentioned (Mitzla) and here numerous relics of Crosses have been discovered both in the possession of the people and among the ruins, chiefly pieces of metal said to be tin, either cut in the shape of Crosses or stamped with the emblem. Some have supposed them to be coins, but it is generally supposed they were also worn as amulets. Wilkinson, in his *Manners and Customs of the Ancient Egyptians*, says that the Egyptians wore the Cross about their persons; and that the Shari, an Assyrian tribe, frequently had a small cross attached to a necklace or to the collar of their dress, also that this custom was not peculiar to the Shari, for the Rotuno, supposed to be Lydians, also wore the Cross figured on their robes, traces of which may be seen in the

Rebo, a Northern Asiatic People resembling Parthians. These instances are adduced to shew that the Cross was in use as early as the 15th century before the Christian era.

It has been shewn also by various writers and travellers that the Scandinavians in the far north also had the Cross, as well as the Scythians, the Celts and the Cymry. In Sweden, likewise, Norway, Russia, Ireland, Cornwall, &c., cruciform excavations have been found.

Mention has been made of the various forms of these Crosses, the ancient and modern pantheons accurately corresponding. A remarkable instance of this is seen in what is called the Maltese Cross, an ornament too well known to need description. It is called Maltese from the circumstance that it was represented in Malta by four huge phalli carved out of the solid granite and which served for the arms; these were afterwards changed by the knights of St. John into the four triangles meeting point downwards at the central globe. The adjacent island of Gozzo had numerous other examples similarly formed, the work of the early Phœnician colonists; the Etruscan and Pompeian monuments represent it in the same grossly conspicuous manner.

It appears in Assyria to have been the emblem chiefly and essentially of royalty, for it is found portrayed on the breasts of the most powerful monarchs of Babylon and Nineveh. It depends with other sacred objects from the necks of many of the kings, and is to be seen on the sculptures in the halls of most of our museums. It represented originally the elysium of the four great gods of the Assyrian Pantheon, Ra, and the first triad Ana, Belus, and Hea; and when inserted in a roundlet was emblematical of Sansi, or the sun dominating the earth as well as the heavens. In Egypt it was sometimes the hieroglyph of goodness, and among the Romans the sign of life. Amongst the former people, by whom it was held specially sacred, it literally abounded; most of the monuments are constantly adorned with it and we find the Ibis represented with human hands and feet, and holding the staff of Ibis in one hand and the globe and cross in the other. In addition Saturn's monogram or symbol was a cross with a ram's horn, Jupiter's a cross with a horn, and Venus's a circle with a cross.

It is a remarkable thing also, that in ancient times in India, buildings erected for heathen worship were constructed, like modern Christian Churches, in the form of Crosses; two of the principal pagodas in that country, viz., those at Benares and Mathura, are thus built.*

Among the stone implements of the shell mounds of Denmark are cruciform hammers, with the hole for the haft at the intersection of the arms, which are of equal length. These were probably used in the sacrifice of victims to Thor, but the Cross of Thor is usually represented as cramponnée, two plain bars equal length, with short right angles at the end crossing in the centres. The hammer of Thor, in form of a Cross, was sometimes used to bless the marriage tie.

Coming nearer home we find the Cross was a common symbol amongst the British, Irish, and Gallic Celts. The shamrock of Ireland derives its sacredness from its resemblance to it in form; and in the mysticism of the Druids the trefoil had a peculiar significance.

From all these examples, and which are but a few of many that might be cited, it is evident that the Cross was a religious symbol common to both Heathens and Christians, and that it was used long before the introduction of Christianity into the world. Its exact meaning, as we have remarked, has always been and probably will remain, more or less, involved in obscurity; this has been a matter of constant dispute and there is no reason to expect that men will ever agree about it. It certainly seems

* Maurice.—*Ind. Antiq. 2.*

an odd fancy that it should be deemed in any way a representative of the male organs of generation, but so it has been, and
thus has been taken to be emblematic of the procreative powers
of nature.   Combining this with the notion that it was the
symbol of eternal life, we get the general idea that it was the
emblem of eternally renovating life.

Respecting this matter, Higgins draws a most remarkable and
evidently untenable conclusion.   He says :—" Nothing in my
opinion can more clearly shew the identity of the two systems
of the Christian priests and of the ancient worshippers of the
Sun than the fact, unquestionably proved, that the sign or monogram used by both was identically the same.   It is absolutely
impossible that this can be the effect of accident."   On the
contrary it strikes some of us that this is an absurd and unwarrant-
able inference.   No attempt, it will be noticed, is made to show
that each used the emblem as representing the same thing.
which it would be impossible to do, but because the emblems
were the same in shape it is argued that the religious systems
were identical.   There are few people so ignorant as not to
know that the Cross of the Christian age refers to the instrument
of death on Calvary, and to nothing else ; this is certain,
whatever was the origin or ultimate signification of the Crosses
of paganism.

The Crux-Ansata.

The most remarkable of all Crosses, and that which excited
the greatest curiosity and amount of discussion, is one common
on the Monuments of Egypt, called the Crux-Ansata, that is,
the Cross with a Handle.   It consists of an Ordinary Cross in
the shape of the Greek *Tau*, or T, with a ring on the top of the
centre, sometimes quite round, but generally of an oval shape,
forming a kind of handle, from which it gets its name Ansata.
From the time of Socrates, Sozomen, and others, for ages in fact,

this symbol has supplied food for the contemplation of the studious and the antiquary, and for the exercise of the ingenuity of the best of scholars. What did it mean? was ever the enquiry, and energetically did everyone urge his arguments who had anything of a theory to offer on the subject. The Egyptian, when called upon for an explanation, simply replied that it (the Tau) was a divine mystery, and a mystery it has always remained. Still, we are in possession of a good many facts and statements relating to it, and from these we select such as may prove of interest.

As we have said, the Crux-Ansata is a common figure on Egyptian Monuments, and is constantly seen in the hands of Isis, Osiris, and other divinities. It can be seen on the sculptures brought from Nineveh, and is clearly marked on the ivory tablets of the Palace of Nimroud; it is also to be seen carved on the walls of the Cave Temples of India.

In the year 389, when the Serapeum at Alexandria was destroyed by order of Theodosius, the Christians, who then first became acquainted with the meaning of the Cross among the Egyptian hieroglyphics, saw in this figure which they found sculptured on the stones a sign prophetic of the coming of Christ, and it is said " They modelled on the same type the symbol of redemption. After this time the Crux-Ansata appears occasionally on Christian Monuments, and some have believed it to be the origin of the monogram of Christ; but that is undoubtedly of an earlier date than the destruction of the temple of Serapis.

It has been contended by some that we have sound historical information relative to the meaning of this symbol, that " It may be considered the only hieroglyphical type concerning whose import we have any certain intelligence." Certain it is that the same astonishment as was exhibited by the Spaniards when they discovered the Cross in America was also exhibited by the Christians at a very early period in ecclesiastical history when they found it frequently recurring among the hieroglyphics of Egypt. Some of the priests who knew the meaning of these hieroglyphics, being converted to Christianity, Dr. Clarke suggests that the secret transpired. The converted heathens, says Socrates Scholasticus, explained the symbol, and declared that it signified "Life to come;" Ruffinus said the same thing. Kircha put the explanation of the Crux-Ansata in a somewhat different manner, but which is said not to militate against the above.

He says it consisted of letters *Phi Tau*, denoting Ptha, a name of Mercury; and the name of this deity, as a conductor of the souls of the dead, might well be used with reference to a state of existence after death. Then Dr. Clarge proceeds to say, that as every Egyptian monogram had its archetype in some animal or instrument of common use, and the original of the crux-ansata seeming to have been a key, we may perhaps, by attending to this curious circumstance, arrive at the original of those allegorical allusions to a key, which, with reference to a future state of existence, are introduced into the Holy Scriptures. Such an allusion is made in the prophecies of Isaiah, concerning the kingdom of Christ (ch. 22 v. 22, "the key of the house of David will I lay upon his shoulder.") Christ said to Peter, "I will give unto thee the keys of the kingdom of heaven," and the author of the Book of Revelation, as if the sacred symbols of ancient Egypt had suggested the image to his mind, describes the Angel of the Resurrection as having in his hand a key. Also in the prophecies concerning the second Advent of the Messiah, a similar allusion may be noticed: "I am He that liveth and was dead, and behold I am alive for evermore, Amen, and have the keys of hell and of death."—(Rev. 1-18.)

Now we get from various scholars and writers, several different opinions respecting the meaning of this remarkable symbol. It has been frequently called the "Key of the Nile," that is to say, it was the representation of the instrument used at the Nileometers for allowing the waters to flow into the neighbouring canals upon the rising of the river to a suitable height. This is endorsed by D. Clarke, Denon, Nordon, and Pocock, and is often put forward in the present day as the true explanation. Then again we have the opinion of Bishop Clogher, who thought it was an agricultural implement used in the process of sowing. Jamblichus thought it was the name of the Divine Being. Various Christian writers conceived the whole figure, or at least the cross, to be expressive of the life to come, deriving this opinion from the explanation given of it by heathen converts who understood the hieroglyphics. The figure is found to vary somewhat in different localities, it sometimes being represented by a cross of four arms with a circle on the top, but more commonly, as we have already described it, as a three-armed cross with the ring in the top in the middle. The circle has been set up by some as emblematic of the Creator and Preserver of the world; as the wisdom derived from him who directs and governs it, is signified by the *Tau*, the monogram of Mercury, Thoth or *Theta Tau*, Ptha.

Then again, others say, we may further suppose it to be the venerable effigy of the supreme deity, which Apuleius informs us, wat not made in the likeness of any creation; or to be the phylactery of Isis, which, not unlike the thummim in the breast-plate of the high-priest, signified, according to Plutarch, the voice of truth. " The learned Therwart," also, says Shaw, " in a very elaborate dissertation, has endeavoured to prove it to be the *acus nautica*, or the mariner's compass, which he supposed was known to the ancients."

Many seem to have endeavoured most persistently to find a Phallic origin both for the Cross simple and for the Crux-Ansata particularly. They thought they saw the union of Osiris and Isis, the active and passive elements in it, and Sir Gardiner Wilkinson noted the remarkable resemblance of the Egyptian word signifying life (ônh) to the *yohni lingam* of the Hindoos.

The lingam-yoni is symbolised by a perpendicular arm rising from the centre of a horizontal one, thus ⊥ indicating the vivifying principal and the reducing principal; reversed, this becomes the famous Tau, or Cross, which was the symbol of life among the Greeks, as *Theta* was of death, being the initial letter of *thanatos* (death).* The Phallic idea seems, if not originated by, to have at least gained strength from the fact that the Cross has been traced from the earliest period of monumental history along with the *equilateral triangle*, the symbol of the generation of all things, of the source of life, of Siva, of Osiris, and of the Trinities in Unity.

One thing, at any rate, seems clear, and that is the inseparable connection between the Cross and the letter Tau—" The earliest form in which this letter occurs is that of a Cross, and such was the meaning of Tau in our ancient customs. In the primitive Hebrew, Numidian, and Greek alphabets, it was represented both as a diagonal and as a rectangular Cross. In the latter Greek alphabet it was the rectangular lingam-yoni symbol reversed." *

There is so much difficulty about the explanation of the origin and meaning of this symbol that we are better able to meet it negatively than otherwise, and to say what it is *not* rather than what it *is*. The Phallic theory has been declared to be " monstrous and devoid of evidence,"† but we are not altogether prepared to denounce thus summarily such a solution, seeing to what an extent Phallism prevails in the east and enters into the composition of the national Ornaments. There is another theory which we need do little more than notice, viz., that which suggests the Tau (T) represents a table or altar, and that the loop symbolises a vase or an egg resting upon it.

* Barlow   † Barton.

Now some very curious things have been said about this *crux-ansata* as the supposed Nile-Key; we may as well say at once that we do not believe it to be anything of the kind, whatever else it may be, or whatever may have been its origin. Sir Gardiner Wilkinson remarks, it is precisely the god Nilus who is least represented with this symbol in his hand, and the Nile-Key is an ascertained figure of different shape. The author of the Hindoo Fragments, however, in discrediting the notion of Bishop Clogher that the crux was a *setting stick* for planting roots and large seeds, evidently leans to the *Key* theory. He says :—"And thus was I, while pondering on these matters, amused by seeing in the hands of the conservators of the city of London, vulgarly called turncocks, an implement almost exactly resembling this classical concern of antiquity. It is the most convenient form that the tool can assume in that class of men, in their round of daily exercise on the banks of the Thames of their useful occupation. And so it was probably in the hands of an equally useful class who had charge of the Nileometers and other matters connected with the rise and distribution of the waters of Egypt. Our turncocks call their tool a key ; and so, perhaps, did the turncocks of the banks of the Nile. One of ours lost, and dug up finely incrustated, two hundred years hence, may puzzle the antiquarians of the day of discovery."

This sounds plausible but the weight of evidence and probability is against it. There is some resemblance certainly between the tool in question, and the crux-ansata, but while the former consists simply of a partially hollow stem with an attached handle, the latter has in addition a conspicuous cross-bar. If such keys were used in Egypt as are used in the London streets for regulating the supply of water to the inhabitants, why are they not found amongst the antiquities of that kingdom? as are other things of an even more perishable nature ; instead of this the Crux-Ansata is found only in painted or sculptured forms upon statues, monuments, and mummy cloths. But when it is called the Nile-Key we are reminded that, were it really such, it would probably have been found only in Egypt; whereas it has been discovered amongst the remains of the ancient cities of Assyria, and in the magnificent cave temples of India. A search amongst the collections in our museums also shews us that it is chiefly found on the wrappings of mummies of persons more or less engaged, centuries ago, in ecclesiastical services. It can be seen for instance in the British Museum on the coverings of incense bearers and priests.

It has been observed, further, that when transferred from Egypt to the alphabets of surrounding nations the *Tau* preserved its sacred character. In Hebrew it retains its name (Thau) and its meaning (a terminus, or cross); and though the figure has at present undergone a change, it is curious that originally it was written as the Greek *Tau*, and in the Samaritan alphabet as an actual Cross, which is "Another stumbling-block in the way of those who consider it to be an implement.*

The more carefully the subject is considered, the more unlikely does it seem that the Crux-Ansata was anything but a religious emblem. In ancient times it was actually borne as an ensign, like that of the latter Roman empire, or those of modern princes. With the lower limb extended, it was the Egyptian banner, and served as a support to the crest or device of their various cities, as a lion for Leontopolis, a goat for Panopolis, &c.

Now there is one very striking piece of evidence that the Tau was a religious emblem, like the Christian Cross, and that is afforded by the singular fact that a great proportion of the Egyptian temples have their ground plan in its form; also, that many of the sekoi were modelled from it, and that it enters largely into the general arrangement of the sepulchral chambers,

* Classical Journal.

In addition, it has been pronounced extraordinary that the Crux-Ansata should be so often seen in symbolical writings, either alone, or held in the hands, or suspended over the necks of deities. Beetles and such other sacred animals and symbols as were bored through and intended for amulets had this figure impressed on them. Show, who speaks thus, declared it to be the same with the " Ineffable image of Eternity " mentioned by Suidas.

The Crux-Ansata is truly a wonderful and mysterious emblem, we could write a volume about its history, but it is doubtful if even then we should have satisfactorily unravelled its full meaning. It it so ancient that we can hardly find the time when it was not, and it is so widely distributed that we light upon it in quarters most unexpected. Whatever it was, everything seems to say it could not have been the supposed " Key of the Nile," far earlier than that it dates, and far more important and sacred was its signification. It has been described as the symbol of symbols, the mystical Tau, the hidden wisdom not only of the ancient Egyptians, but also of the Chaldeans, Phœnicians, Mexicans, and Peruvians, and of every other ancient people commemorated in history, in either hemisphere. As our letter T with a roundlet or oval above, it was figured on the gigantic emerald or glass statue of Serapis, which was transported, B.C. 293, by order of Ptolemy Soter from Sinope, on the shores of the Black Sea, re-erected within the labyrinth which compassed banks of Lake Mœris, and destroyed by the victorious army of Theodosius in A.D. 389, despite the earnest entreaties of the Egyptian priesthood to spare it because it was the emblem of their God and of the life to come. Strangely enough, " as in the oldest temples and catacombs of Egypt, so this type likewise abounds in the ruined cities of Mexico and Central America, graven as well upon the most ancient cyclopean and polygonal walls as upon the more modern and perfect examples of masonry ;

and is displayed in an equally conspicuous manner upon the
breasts of innumerable bronze statuettes which have been disin-
terred from the cemetery of Jingalpa—of unknown antiquity—in
Nicaragua." *

So universal is the belief in the antiquity of the tau or cross,
that it is supposed by the best scholars to have been the mark
which the children of Israel made on the door-posts of their
houses by order of Moses, that, in the destruction of the first-
born of the land of Egypt, the angel of death might see it, and
pass over them. It is also supposed, indeed taken for granted, to
be the mark of salvation, spoken of by Ezekiel (ch. 9 v. 4), to be
set on the foreheads of the men who were not to be slain.

Like the Christian Cross, which in so many ways has been
displayed in old architectural ornaments and early coins, the
Crux-Ansata appears in simple uncompounded state or in the
most complicated forms, and is the origin of those beautiful
scrolls called Greek and Etruscan, but which are in reality
Egyptian.

Evidently, we think, it was unmistakeably a religious emblem,
venerated equally with the modern crosses of Christianity, an
emblem at once the most ancient and the most mysterious of any
to be met with. Phallic in some way it may have been, especially
as it is found painted and engraved upon those parts of the
human body by whose action the race is multiplied and preserved,
and entering into the composition of figures combining the sexes
of both male and female. Even if we take this view of it, it will
in no way militate against the further opinion that " while the
Christian Cross is the record of an historical miracle, the Crux-
Ansata must be considered as the memento of some predicted
benefit to man."

* Classical Journal.

CHAPTER VII.

*The Hebrews and Phallism—Solomon and the Heathen Gods—
Old Testament Characters—Worship in Groves—Consecrated
Pillars—Asherah and the Grove—Ashtoreth—Jewish Lingham
— Iniquity of Solomon — Worship of Baal — St. Jerome on
Baal-Peor—Jewish Opinion of Baal-Peor—Maachah's Idol.*

THERE are some passages in the Old Testament Scriptures
bearing upon this subject as it relates to the people of
Israel, and a brief notice of the same and the matters they reveal
will not be out of place. To recite them they read as follows : —
In I. Kings, ch. 11, v. 5, " For Solomon went after Ashtoreth
the goddess of the Sidonians, and after Milcom the abomination
of the Ammonites "; v. 33, " They have forsaken me, and have
worshipped Ashtoreth the goddess of the Sidonians, Chemosh the
god of the Moabites, and Milcom the god of the children of
Ammon." And again in II. Kings, ch. 23, v. 13, " And the high
places that were on the right hand of the mount of corruption,
which Solomon the King of Israel had builded for Ashtoreth the
abomination of the Sidonians, and for Chemosh the abomination
of the Moabites, and for Milcom the abomination of the children
of Ammon, did the King defile. And he (Josiah) brake in pieces
the images and cut down the groves, and filled their places with
the bones of men."

We are introduced here most undeniably to a certain species
of the most abominable idolatry on the part of Solomon and
others who lived under his rule, and from certain considerations
which we now propose to offer, we shall probably arrive at the
conclusion that it partook largely of the nature of sex worship.
This may startle some who have been accustomed to regard many

of these Old Testament characters as patterns of all that is simple
and virtuous, but facts are stubborn things, and we are faced in
the passages quoted with the honest revelation of Scripture itself,
that Solomon was led away from his rightful undivided allegiance
to the God of his forefathers, and "went after Ashtoreth the
goddess of the Sidonians and other abominations." A mention is
made also of the groves which had been constructed by the
idolators for the purposes of this unhallowed worship, and which
Josiah the new and righteous king cut down and destroyed.

It is an ascertained fact that ages ago the heathen carried on
their worship of the unknown God entirely, or almost entirely,
in the open air. The sun was their principal deity, and as no
temple could be imagined extensive enough to enclose him, they
adored him outside all walls of any description saying, "the
whole world is a temple for the sun." Even in after ages when
buildings for worship had been erected and were fast multiplying,
there were certain deities, such as Terminus for instance, who
were always adored in temples which were left without a covering
or roof. So sprang up the custom of choosing hills and mountains, on which they thought the sacrifices were more acceptable
because they considered they were nearer to God. From early
simplicity, as we point out in another place, idolatry grew complicated and mystical and the gods increased to an enormous
extent, and numberless hills were set apart and consecrated for
the service. Here they planted trees in thick masses and
avenues, forming the shady and secluded groves which we read
so much of in ancient historians. Chiefly, however, were such
places created, on account of the growing impurity of the heathen
rites, and it was rather that they might indulge unmolested in
their carnal orgies, than from any religious convictions that they
resorted to the solitude of the leafy grove. Such places were
made to look as much as possible like natural temples or the
shrines of particular divinities, and by adorning the trees with

lights and ribbons, and dedicating certain of them to one or another of the gods, they continued to foster and intensify the belief that they were peculiarly sacred. In these books of the Old Testament, as well as in Hebrew historians of days long gone by, we get very plain statements of the Jewish failings in their allegiance to God and the going of the people after other deities. The temptation to construct these woods and groves was too much for them in spite of all the injunctions and enactments of their law-givers to destroy such things whenever they came across them, and though they had seen the severest judgments fall upon those who had given way to the desire, and had felt the divine displeasure on account of their own idolatry, they repeated again and again their preposterous idolatry and opposition to the law. The writings of the prophets are full of denunciation of these sins, and Maimonides describes the idolatrous objects which they multiplied and set up in all sorts of places, public and private. Lewis says :—" The most ancient monuments of idolatry among the Gentiles were consecrated pillars or columns, which the Hebrews were forbidden to erect as objects of divine homage and adoration. This practice is conceived to have arisen from an imitation of Jacob, who took a stone and set it up for a pillar, as a monument of the divine mercy to him, and to preserve the memory of the vision which he had seen. This stone was held in great veneration in future times, and by the Jews removed to Jerusalem ; after the destruction of which by Titus, they were indulged (upon that day when it was taken, which was the only day they were permitted to come thither) with great lamentation and expressions of sorrow, to go anoint this stone. From the word Bethel, the place where the pillar was erected, came the word *bat'ylia* among the heathen, which signified *rude stones*, which they worshipped either as symbols of divinity, or as true gods animated by some heavenly power." *

* *Origines Hebreæ.*

H

Now it seems very probable indeed that the erection of the pillar of Jacob originated the worship of the Phallus among the people of that part of the world, " for," continues Lewis, " the learned Bochael asserts that the Phœnicians, at least as the Jews think, first worshipped this very stone which Jacob anointed, and afterwards consecrated others, which they called *bætylia* or *bætyli*, in memory of this stone anointed at Bethel.   It is certain that this idolatrous custom came very early into the world, which gave occasion to Moses, not only to forbid the erecting of such pillars, but to command them to be broken down and destroyed, whenever they were found, because in his time they were converted to profane uses."

The similarity between this anointing and the pouring of oil upon phallic objects, as we have described, in India, both in ancient and modern times, is remarkable.

It is difficult not to believe that the Hebrew grove worship was anything else than the Phallic worship we have been describing. Grove is the English translation of the Hebrew word Asherah. As to what this Asherah was, there has been much disputing, but upon some things scholars have been pretty unanimous.   Dr. Smith's dictionary says, " Asherah, the name of a Phœnician goddess, or rather of the idol itself."   Our translators following the rendering of the LXX. (*aldos*) and of the Vulg (*lucus*) translated the word by ' grove.'   Almost all modern interpreters however since Selden, agree that an idol or image of some kind must be intended, as seems sufficiently proved from such passages as II. Kings, 21, v. 7 ; and 23, v. 6, in the latter of which we find that Josiah, ' brought out the Asherah ' (or as our version reads, ' the grove ') ' from the house of the Lord.' "   There can moreover be no doubt that Asherah is very closely connected with Ashtoreth and her worship, indeed the two are so placed in connection with each other, and each of them with Baal (*c.g.* Judg. 2, v. 7, Comp. 2, v. 3, Judg. 6, v. 25, I. Kings 18, v. 19), that many critics have regarded them as identical. There are other passages however in which these terms seem to be distinguished from each other. Movers first pointed out and established the difference between the two names, though he probably goes too far in considering them as names of distinct deities. The view maintained by Berthau, appears to be the more correct one, that Ashtoreth is the proper name of the goddess, whilst Asherah is the name of the image or symbol of the goddess. This symbol seems in all cases to have been of wood (see *c.g.* Judg. 6, v. 25-30, and II. Kings, 23, v. 14), and the most probable etymology of the term indicates that is was formed of the straight stem of a tree, whether living or set up for the purpose, and thus points us to the phallic rites with which no doubt the worship of Astarte was connected."

If we turn to other learned sources of information we find very similar conclusions arrived at as those just mentioned, and there are passages in Kitto's Cyclopædia from which we make selections, entirely in countenance with what has been stated.

" As for the power of nature which was worshipped under the name of Ashtoreth, Creuser and Münter assert that it was the principle of conception and parturition—that subordinate power which fecundated by a superior influence, but which is the agent of all births throughout the universe. As such, Münter maintains, in his *Religion der Babylonier*, in opposition to the remarks of Gesenius, that the original form under which Ashtoreth was worshipped was the *moon*; and that the transition from that to the *planet* Venus, was unquestionably an innovation of a later date. It is evident that the moon alone can be properly called the queen of heaven; as also that the dependent relation of the moon to the sun makes it a more appropriate symbol of that sex, whose functions as female and mother throughout the whole extent of animated nature, were embodied in Ashtoreth. As for the places consecrated to her worship, although the numerous passages in which the authorised version has erroneously given *grove* are to be deducted, there are yet several occasions on which *gardens* and *shady trees* are mentioned as peculiar seats of (probably *her*) lascivious rites. As to the form and attributes with which Ashtoreth was represented, the oldest known image, that in Paphos, with a white conical stone, often seen on Phœnician remains in the figure which Tacitus describes, Münter is unwilling to consider this a Lingham symbol, nevertheless there appears to be some room for disputing his opinion."

This then was what Solomon did, he went after Astaroth, the impure Venus of the Sidonians; after Milcom, the abomination of the Ammonites; after Chemosh, the abomination of the Moabites; and after the murderous Moloch, the abomination of the children of Ammon. "He seems," says Adam Clarke, "to have gone as far in iniquity as it was possible." And all these were worshipped upon what the Old Testament in II. Kings, 23, v. 5, calls "the high places before Jerusalem, which were on the right hand of the mount of Corruption."

Concealed in the shadow of a feeble translation, the misdeeds of the once wise king look comparatively mild and tame, but exposed to the glare of a fierce and keen criticism, come out in all their horribleness. "Solomon loved many strange women, together with the daughter of Pharaoh, women of the Moabites, Ammonites, Edomites, Sidonians, and Hittites, of the nations concerning which the Lord said unto the children of Israel, ye shall not go into them, neither shall they come in unto you: for surely they will turn away your heart after their gods: Solomon clave unto these in love. And he had seven hundred wives, princesses, and three hundred concubines; and his wives turned away his heart." * And so he took up with the filthy and

---

* Kings, XI., 1—3.

abominable deities of the heathen, Chemosh, Milcom, Sun and Fire, the worship of the regenerative energies of nature — the worship of the impure god of love, and the Mount of Olives and the front of Jerusalem were polluted with his Phallic emblems, pillars and altars.

In like manner as Ashtoreth was the moon was the abominable Baal the sun. " In a certain sense any argument which goes to shew that Ashtoreth was the moon is also, on account of the close conjunction between her and Baal, as valid a reason for Baal being the sun ; for the two gods are such exact correlates, that the discovery of the true meaning of the one would lead by the force of analogy, to that of the other." *

Now we are informed in the Book of Numbers (ch. 25, &c.), and in many other places, also by ancient Jewish writers, that the Hebrews rendered divine honours to the god Baal Peor. St. Jerome who was aware of this both from scripture and from tradition, mentions this and calls him the Priapus of the Greeks and Romans. He says he was principally worshipped by women " *colentibus maxime faeminis Baal Phegor, ob obscaeni magnitudinem, quem nos Priapum possumus appellare.*

Maimonides affirms that the adoration paid to this idol consisted in discovering the *mons veneris* before it.

It is a very ancient tradition indeed among the Jews of all ages that this idol was a particularly obscene deity, whose figure, and the manner of worshipping it, was filthy and abominable.

The prophet Hosea in chap. 9, v. 10, says, " I found Israel like grapes in the wilderness : I saw your fathers as the first ripe in the fig tree at her first time ; but they went to Baal Peor, and separated themselves unto that shame." From this the Jews have always held that the god was served by an obscene act which required his worshippers to be uncovered before him, as

* Kitto.

Maimonides says to exhibit their secret parts; hence the law commanding the priests to wear drawers when sacrificing, and their being forbidden to go up to the altar by steps lest their persons should happen to be uncovered.

The Talmudists are also of opinion that the figure was grossly obscene, *imago virilis membri cui quotidi incquibat.*

It is not to be forgotten also that from this god one of the mountains of the Moabites, viz., Pehor, derives its name, it is concluded therefore, that he was there worshipped, and so was a rural god. Such was Priapus, as may be seen in Catullus and Tibullus quoted in the proper place.

" It is evident further," says Lewis, " that fornification was in a manner consecrated to this filthy deity; the Israelites joining themselves to Baalpeor, and at the same time committting whoredom with the daughters of Moab, which may be said likewise of Priapus, who was made *membrosior æquo* only to signify his lasciviousness; and therefore in those infamous epigrams called *Priapæia* or Lusus in *Priapum,* he is called *deus salax.*"

Kitto follows in much the same strain with " It is the common opinion that this god was worshipped by obscene rites, and from the time of Jerome downwards it has been usual to compare him to Priapus. Most Jewish authorities (except the Targum of Jonathan on Num. xxv.) represent his worship to have consisted of rites which are filthy in the extreme, but not lascivious. If it could be shewn that this God was worshipped by libidinous rites it would be one more confirmation of the relation between Baal and the sun, as then Baal Peor would be a masculine phasis of the same worship as that of which Mylitta is, both in name and rites, the female representative."

The more the subject is studied the blacker becomes the tale of the Jewish idolatry and the more evident the fact of its being of a phallic character. It is as wonderful as it is painful, to read in the Book of the Kings, the amount of testimony to this effect, and we are struck at once with the candour and outspoken honesty of the Sacred Historians. If we turn to I. Kings XIV., 24, XV. 12, 13, XXII. 46; and II. Kings, XXIII., 7, we find conspicuous samples of the thing we are describing. It is said that Maachah "made an idol in a grove," and Dr. Clarke commenting upon the passage says, "It is pretty evident" (after quoting Rabbi Solomon Jarchi's testimony that she made it *ad instar membri virilis*, and other authorities from the Chaldee, Arabic, Hebrew, and Greek) " that the image was a mere Priapus, or something of the same nature, and that Maachah had an assembly in the grove where this image was set up, and doubtless worshipped it with the most impure rites."

It is a somewhat singular thing that the Septuagint, in many places, interprets the word Baal with a feminine article, and so makes it representative of a goddess as well as a god. Lewis says it is difficult to discover in the Hebrew text, any reason for this notion of the Judaized Greeks, for (if I mistake not) Baal in the Hebrew is always masculine; but doubtless they had learnt by the Phœnician tradition, that there was a goddess as well as a god of that name. Arnobius observes, that Baal was of an uncertain sex, and his votaries, when they called upon him, invoked him thus: " Hear us, whether thou art a god or a goddess;" and the reason why the heathens made their gods hermaphrodites of both sexes, was to express the generative and prolific virtue of the deity.

The facts we have just been narrating, added to others mentioned in the course of this book, shew us that Phallic worship of the most debasing character prevailed amongst the Jews in the olden time, affecting even their monarch and highest nobles, and leading to practices filthy, abominable, and destructive.

So ends, for the present, our review of this remarkable and interesting subject. It remains with the public to say whether in the future we resume it, and deal with some of the other phases of it which careful researches have brought to light. A large amount of material is at our disposal, and it is possible to render a good deal of information about what has always been considered too mystical to be explained. It is not, we remark in closing, a subject belonging only to the past; Phallic worship still prevails in the East. In the temples of Siva, the Phallus, crowned with flowers and surmounted by a golden star, is exposed in the sanctuary, and lamps are kept burning before it. Offerings of Phalli are still made in the Buddhist temples by barren women, just as they were by the Roman wives in the temple of Venus. These are sufficient reasons for continuing our study, and seeking to understand the theology of our eastern brothers.

THE END.

AUTHORITIES.

Knight's Symbolical Language of Ancient Art.
Westropp's Symbol Worship.
O'Brien's Round Towers of Ireland.
Dean's Serpent Worship.
M'Clintock's Encyclopædia.
Fergusson's Serpent Worship.
Higgins's Anacalypsis.
Inman's Ancient Faiths.
Petrie's Round Towers of Ireland.
Forlong's Rivers of Life.
Baring Gould's Origin of Religious Beliefs.
Herodotus.
Moor's Hindoo Pantheon.
Moor's Oriental Fragments.
Maurice's Indian Antiquities.
Athenæus.
Aristophanes.
Diodorus Siculus.
Barlow's Essays on Symbolism.
Mitra's Antiquities of Orissa.
Forbes's Oriental Memoirs.
Classical Journal.
Barth's Religions of India.
Tiele's History of Egyptian Religion.
Haslam's Cross and the Serpent.
Baring Gould's Curious Myths of the Middle Ages.
Clarke's Travels.
Shaw's Travels.
Lewis's Origines Hebreæ.

Gorious' Etruscan Antiquities.
Sellon's Annotations of Sacred Books of Hindoos.
Renouf's Hibbert Lectures for 1879.
Bonwick's Egyptian Beliefs.
Banier's Mythology of the Ancients.
Seeley's Wonders of Ellora.
Legge's Chinese Classics.
Alabaster's Modern Buddhist.
Beale's Legend of Buddha.
Edkins's Chinese Buddhism.
Huc's Travels.
Cust's Pictures of Indian Life.
Wilson's Essays on Hinduism.
Monier Williams' Hinduism.
Coleman's Mythology of the Hindus.
Burgess's Elephanta.
Rawlinson's Ancient Monarchies.
Faber's Origin of Pagan Idolatry.
Hislop's Two Babylons.
Fergusson's Palaces of Nineveh.
Layard's Nineveh.
Cory's Ancient Fragments.
Cory's Mythological Enquiries.
Took's Pantheon.
Oort's Worship of Baalim.
Catullus.
Tibullus.
Archæological Soc. Journals.
Horace.
Anthropological Soc. Journals.
Asiatic Researches.
Rawlinson's Ancient Egypt.
Gumpach's Historical Antiquities of Egypt.
Osburn's Monumental Egypt.
Osburn's Antiquities of Egypt.
Wilkinson's Ancient Egypt.
Kenrick's Ancient Egypt.
Higgins's Druids.
Smiddy's Druids and Towers of Ireland.
Borlase's Antiquities of Cornwall.
Rimmer's Ancient Stone Crosses.
Tacitus.

Propertius.
Lucan Pharsalia.
Prescott's Conquest of Mexico.
Picard's Religious Ceremonies.
Rollin's Ancient History.
Fergusson and Burgess, Cave Temples.
Waring's Monuments and Ornaments.
Sacred Books of the East.
Oliver's Initiation into Ancient Rites.
Bhlavatsky's Isis Unveiled.

www.ingramcontent.com/pod-product-compliance
Lightning Source LLC
Chambersburg PA
CBHW032111010726
47493CB00008B/2538